MW01595473

7 Keys To Learning Windows NT

Forrest Houlette

NEW RIDERS
PUBLISHING

New Riders Publishing,
Carmel, Indiana

7 Keys To Learning Windows NT

By Forrest Houlette

Published by:

New Riders Publishing
11711 N. College Ave., Suite 140
Carmel, IN 46032 USA

Printed in the United States of America 1 2 3 4 5 6 7 8 9 0

Library of Congress Cataloging-in-Publication Data

Houlette, Forrest, 1954-
7 Keys To Learning Windows NT /Forrest Houlette.
    p. cm.
    Includes index.
    ISBN 1-56205-156-3
    1. Operating systems (Computers) 2. Windows NT.
    I. Title.
QA76.76.063H68 1993   93-13744
005.4'469—dc20   CIP

Publisher
Lloyd J. Short

Associate Publisher
Tim Huddleston

Acquisitions Manager
Cheri Robinson

Acquisitions Editor
Rob Tidrow

Managing Editor
Matthew Morrill

Marketing Manager
Brad Koch

Product Director
Mike Groh

Production Editor
Nancy E. Sixsmith

Editors
Margaret Berson, Mary Ann Larguier, Steve Weiss

Technical Editors
Mark Hripko

Acquisitions Coordinator
Stacey Beheler

Editorial Secretary
Karen Opal

Publishing Assistant
Melissa Keegan

Book Design and Production
Lisa Daugherty, Dennis Clay Hager, Carla Hall-Batton,
Mike Mucha, Juli Pavey, Angela Pozdol, Michelle Self,
Barbara Webster, Alyssa Yesh

Proofreaders
Terri Edwards, Mitzi Foster Gianakos, Howard Jones,
Sean Medlock, Tonya Simpson, Marcella Thompson,
Dennis Wesner, Donna Winter

Indexed by
Joelynn Gifford, John Sleeva

Trademark Acknowledgments

New Riders Publishing has made every attempt to supply trademark information about company names, products, and services mentioned in this book. Trademarks indicated below were derived from various sources. New Riders Publishing cannot attest to the accuracy of this information.

Warning and Disclaimer

This book is designed to provide information about the Windows NT computer program. Every effort has been made to make this book as complete and as accurate as possible, but no warranty or fitness is implied.

The information is provided on an "as is" basis. The author and New Riders Publishing shall have neither liability nor responsibility to any person or entity with respect to any loss or damages arising from the information contained in this book or from the use of the disks or programs that may accompany it.

Table of Contents

Part 2 Learning Windows NT Basics

Part 3 Managing Applications

Part 4 Mastering Key Windows NT Tools

Part 5 Managing Files

9   File Manager 239

10   File and Disk Management 263

Part 6 Printing

Part 7 Troubleshooting

Introduction

7 Keys to Learning Windows NT provides an instant resource for the Windows NT workstation user. This book can help increase your productivity and decrease the time it takes to do tasks. It presents information the same way Windows does—in a visual, intuitive, and easy-to-understand format. Kept close to your computer, 7 Keys to Learning Windows NT can provide the immediate information you need to perform a wide range of Windows NT tasks. Each chapter's "Notes" section includes hints for optimizing your work in the Windows NT environment, and a chapter on "Troubleshooting" serves as a convenient and comprehensive problem-solving guide.

Who Should Use 7 Keys to Learning Windows NT?

Many people who use Windows, whether occasionally or daily, need help to remember the most efficient way to perform a task. They also appreciate learning new shortcuts and tips for improved performance. With the arrival of Windows NT, even frequent users of Windows 3.1 and Windows for Workgroups face mastering new tasks unique to the secure NT environment. *7 Keys to Learning Windows NT* meets the needs of a wide range of Windows users, including:

- Those who use the Windows interface infrequently, no matter which versions, and who must occasionally use Windows NT

- Those who use some aspects of Windows frequently, but other features rarely

- Beginners who need a simple and easy-to-use reference for performing specific tasks

- Curious users who want to explore the Windows NT environment

- Experienced Windows users who seek to improve their efficiency and learn new Windows NT skills

- Those who must switch among the various Windows versions frequently

Windows beginners will find *7 Keys to Learning Windows NT* to be an ideal companion to New Riders' *Inside Windows NT* tutorial reference to Windows. Intermediate and advanced Windows users will find *7 Keys to Learning Windows NT* to be a quick-to-use task reference supplement to any other Windows NT book.

What is Included in *7 Keys to Learning Windows NT*?

Features designed into this unique reference include the following:

- Referenced step-by-step instructions that show you how to perform each essential task in Windows NT

- Tips and notes that you can use to improve your efficiency

- Cautions to help you avoid common problems

How are the Tasks Organized?

7 Keys to Learning Windows NT is organized into seven main parts. The chapters in each part group related tasks together to help you find the information you need. To determine which chapter is most likely to help you, think about your overall objective. Are you setting up Windows NT? Are you customizing features? Are you working with a DOS, OS/2, or POSIX application? Or are you troubleshooting?

The first page of a chapter lists the tasks presented in that chapter. Each task begins by describing the reasons for performing the task in the segment called "When To Use." The next part of the task description, "Steps To Follow," shows you exactly how to perform the task. The elements that you must use for each step are discussed, and the required actions are clearly explained. The final portion of the task description presents "Notes" about shortcuts, cautions, extending the task, and increasing performance. The final pages of this book contain a comprehensive index of the topics covered within the text.

The following descriptions are provided to help you locate the information you want:

Part One: Getting Windows NT Started

Chapter 1, "Planning for Windows NT," explains new concepts that are introduced in Windows NT that affect the way you organize and use your system.

Chapter 2, "Windows NT Setup," outlines installing and configuring Windows. You learn about setting up your system, using and optimizing memory, and managing network connections.

Chapter 3, "Log-on and Administrative Tasks," explains key features of Windows NT security, including logging on, setting up user accounts, and monitoring your system for security problems.

Part Two: Learning Windows NT Basics

Chapter 4, "Windows NT Basics," gives an overview of general Windows NT concepts and procedures, such as using the keyboard, the mouse, and the Control menu.

Chapter 5, "Customizing Windows NT," outlines ways to customize Windows NT to suit your appearance and performance preferences. You learn to change desktop colors, features, and setup defaults.

Part Three: Managing Applications

Chapter 6, "Program Manager," tells you how to add programs to the Windows NT environment and how to control program groups and program items.

Chapter 7, "DOS, OS/2, and POSIX Applications," explains how to work with DOS, OS/2, and POSIX applications. You learn how Windows handles files and how applications that are written for these other operating systems work in conjunction with Windows NT.

Part Four: Mastering Key Windows NT Tools

Chapter 8, "Windows NT Tools," gives an overview of the various tools that are provided with Windows NT. In this chapter, you learn about tools that can make you more productive, including Clipboard Viewer, Windows Help, Character Map, Recorder, Dynamic Data Exchange, macros, and the Edit menu.

Part Five: Managing Files

Chapter 9, "File Manager," outlines how to use the File Manager program to operate and navigate your Windows NT system.

Chapter 10, "File and Disk Management," tells you how to organize your Windows NT desktop and filing system. This chapter deals with formatting and labeling disks, creating and managing directories, performing file actions, connecting to network drives, and managing file security.

Part Six: Printing

Chapter 11, "Printing," discusses the use of printers with Windows NT. You learn about adding and removing printers, configuring printers, working with network printers, and using Print Manager to control print jobs.

Chapter 12, "Troubleshooting," describes various problems you can encounter, and offers suggestions to resolve them. You find information on dealing with configuration files, solving Windows NT installation and configuration problems, improving program performance, fixing printer problems, and making the communication ports work properly.

Windows NT Basics

Three mouse actions help you carry out the steps for each task: *pointing*, *clicking*, and *double-clicking*. To point, move the mouse until the pointer on the screen is aimed at the desired location. To click, point the mouse pointer at an object and press the mouse button once. (As with all mouse actions in Windows NT, use the left mouse button to perform this action, unless you have switched the roles of the mouse buttons by using the Control Panel.) To double-click, point the mouse pointer to an object and rapidly press the mouse button twice.

Several graphical objects help you to follow the steps in each task. *Icons*, small pictures that represent programs, are shown as they appear on your screen. Each icon can be opened to reveal the program it represents by double-clicking on it or by pressing the Enter key after the icon is highlighted. (You can move the highlighter with the Alt-Tab key combination, the Ctrl-Tab key combination, or the arrow keys. Use the method that works for the icon you want to open.)

The types of icons and the action that occurs when they are opened are as follows:

- **Application icon**. Loads the application represented, which appears on the screen ready for you to use

- **Document icon**. Opens within the appropriate application, and presents a document ready for you to edit

- **Group icon**. In the Program Manager application, shows the new group of program item icons, and waits for you to select the next step

- **Program Item icon**. In Program Manager, loads the application represented, which appears on the screen ready for you to use

Group icon   Program item icon

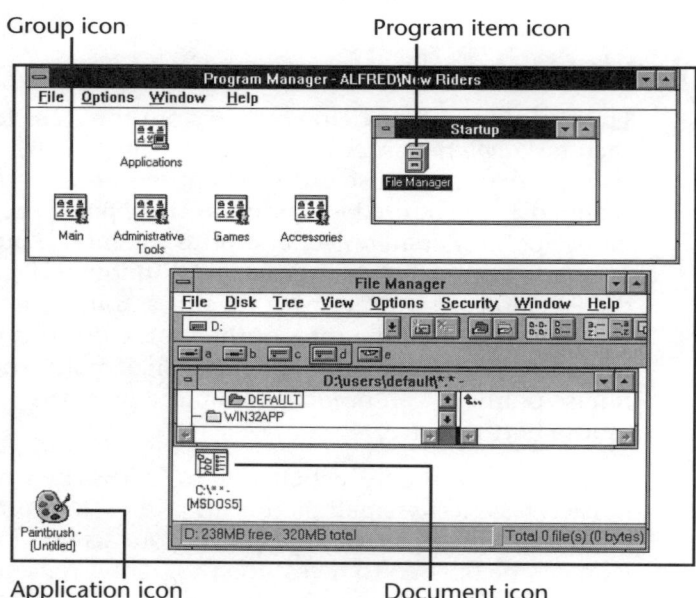

Application icon   Document icon

Part One:

Getting Windows NT Started

Planning for Windows NT

Windows NT Setup

Log-on and Administrative Tasks

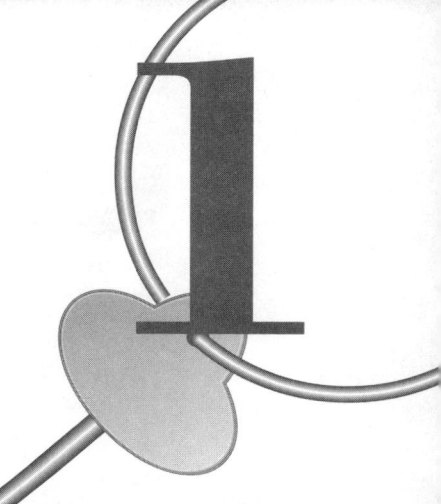

Planning for Windows NT

Windows NT can be set up straight from the box by inserting the disk or CD and powering up your computer. The Setup program leads you through all the necessary decisions, and provides you with a functional NT system. You will notice several differences between Windows NT and other systems as soon as you use it for the first time after installation. For example, Windows NT expects you to log in to your own system by using a password. This difference and others make the time spent planning your Windows NT system very valuable. A bit of planning will make using your computer with Windows NT much more productive.

Because Windows NT provides system security, supports multiple operating systems, and supports multiple file systems, you need to answer the following five questions to plan an optimal installation of Windows NT:

- Who will control my computer?

- Who will use my computer?

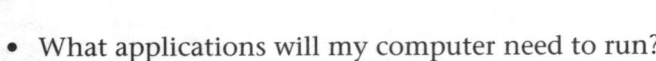

- What applications will my computer need to run?
- What file systems do I need to access?
- How many operating systems do I need on my computer?

This chapter explores the issues relevant to each of these questions, and gives an explanation of who needs to consider each question.

Who Will Control My Computer?

When To Use

Each user of Windows NT needs to know the answer to this question. Most likely, you are used to controlling your system. Because of Windows NT security, however, complete control of your system may be delegated to someone else, and you may not be given complete rights over your own computer. This section explains why and how to make the decision of who should control the computer.

Notes

Windows NT forces you to designate an administrator for your system during installation. The *administrator* is the person who has full control of the computer system. You must decide who this person will be before you begin the setup process. After setup begins, Windows NT asks this designated administrator to enter a password that must remain confidential.

Ideally, the administrator should specify a password during setup, log in as soon after setup as possible, and then change her password. This is the most secure procedure.

The administrator of a system must be a trusted member of your organization, with solid integrity and good working habits relating to security matters. Trust is important, because this individual will have full charge of all applications and data on the system, including the capability of intentionally erasing or altering data. Integrity is important because you probably have proprietary, mission-critical data stored on the system.

Good working habits are important because all security procedures tend to become lax over time. The administrator must be someone who can maintain the highest degree of vigilance possible while dealing with the routine, repetitive administrative tasks that can lull even the best of workers into a false sense of security.

The administrator must enforce security at the administrative level of the system. The administrator's password should not be written down. If it is, it must be kept under lock and key, and should not be easily guessed.

Passwords that contain words that run together, such as BlowTheDuckOver; or words separated by numbers or punctuation marks, such as Love30PotBelliedPigs, offer great security. So do passwords that contain foreign words.

If the administrator's password is forgotten, the only solution is to reinstall Windows NT and specify a new administrative password on installation.

Because the reinstallation of Windows NT gives a new administrator access to the system, the administrator must take reasonable care that an unscrupulous individual does not have the capability of reinstalling the operating system. Windows NT installation disks should be kept under lock and key, and you may want to disable booting from a floppy disk if it is possible to

do so on your system. You can also install a hardware-level password if your system's ROM allows this capability.

WARNING   Certain actions, such as disabling boot from floppy and installing a hardware-level password, can have unpleasant side effects. This is especially true if there is ever an operating system-level problem that prevents you from booting your system. If you cannot boot the system, and cannot enter the ROM setup program, you may have a computer that cannot be booted except with the assistance of a factory technician. Pursuing this level of security has to be weighed against the possible problems and downtime in the event of a boot failure.

Who Will Use My Computer?

When To Use

The answer to this question is probably "you." Most computers in an organization are used by several individuals, however. Although there is one primary user—the person on whose desk the computer sits—many others may sit down at the keyboard and use the computer. A coworker, for instance, may be one of those individuals. The members of your workgroup may also spend time at your keyboard, no matter how briefly, by using programs and accessing the data on your drive. You may even ask other people to do work on your computer for you.

Because Windows NT enforces security requirements, you need to know which users will access your computer and what they will do on it. You can create several log-on accounts so that each user can have appropriate access to your computer. This section explains how to answer the question of who will use your computer, and what rights these people should be given.

Notes

You should list the users of your computer and what they do when they use it. If you do not know, keep a log next to your keyboard for a week, and have each user sign in, note the tasks he performed, and list the software he used. This log will tell you how to organize Windows NT log-in accounts on your system.

You need to determine to which directories and which files each user needs access, and you must know whether any of your computer's users needs access to your network. You can determine directory needs from the applications that each person uses and where you store the files to which she needs access.

Access to the network can be determined by whether a user uses files, directories, or applications on a network drive; and by whether the user needs access to capabilities that are available only over the network, such as electronic mail.

Windows NT enables you to establish log-on accounts for each user of your system. It provides one account, the Guest account, for occasional users who need little access to anything except your company's most widespread applications.

You should establish a separate account for users who need greater access. Such accounts, named after the user, store the user's desktop and screen preferences, and enforce the level of security you decide to grant. You can allow each user access to only the applications, files, and directories to which he needs access.

TIP There is another good reason for establishing a log-on account for each user of your system. When security problems occur, you can lock out all other users.

If you are not your system's administrator, but you are its primary user, ask your administrator to grant you the right to create log-on accounts with limited privileges. You can then create and delete log-on accounts as you need them. You have control over the log-ons you create, but not those created by the administrator. You therefore have little chance of damaging system security by accident while creating or deleting log-ons.

What Applications Will My Computer Need To Run?

When To Use

Before you purchased Windows NT, the answer to this question was "the applications for the operating system installed on my computer." With Windows NT, however, the number of applications that your computer can run is larger. You can run DOS applications, Windows applications, POSIX applications, and OS/2 applications. In addition, you may not want all users of your computer to have access to every application you have installed. This section explores ways to select applications and how to decide to give access to applications to users.

Notes

You should make a list of all the applications you have installed on your computer prior to installing Windows NT. Some applications on this list may become obsolete when you install Windows NT because Windows NT provides their functionality. The backup program that you used prior to installing Windows NT is a good example. You may want to add some applications that you previously used on someone else's computer because it ran another operating system that Windows NT now supports for you. (A POSIX-compliant database is a good example.)

You must decide who will have access to each application. In Windows NT, you can decide that each user of your system can have access to only a limited range of the applications available. (To set such limitations, you must use the NT file system.) Once you have determined who can use your system, determine the access that each person should have to your applications. You can set this access by using the File Manager, according to the groups to which the user belongs.

Chapter 3 explains more about groups, and Chapter 10 discusses ways to grant a user access rights.

What File Systems Do I Need To Access?

When to Use

The question of which file system to use has not been much of an issue before—you used the file system that matched the operating system you had installed. Windows NT, however, supports three file systems: FAT (File Allocation Table), used by MS-DOS; HPFS (High-Performance File System), used by OS/2; and NTFS (NT File System), used by Windows NT exclusively. This section helps you decide which of these file systems to use with your installation of Windows NT.

Notes

No matter what you decide, you will always use the MS-DOS FAT file system with Windows NT because this is the file system that Windows NT uses with floppy disks. When you format a floppy disk (or store information on one), Windows NT uses FAT to ensure that another computer can read the information. As a result, you can easily exchange information among the computers in your organization. No matter which operating system they use, these computers should recognize FAT floppy disks.

Which file system do you want to use on your hard drive(s)? The answer depends on two issues: security and compatibility. If your primary concern is maintaining security on your system, you should choose the NT file system, which enables you to set access privileges on individual directories and files.

 Although you must use NTFS to enforce directory and file-level security, you can take advantage of the Windows NT security features that are managed through log-on accounts with any file system.

When you must maintain multiple operating systems on your computer, you cannot easily convert to NTFS because the other operating systems cannot recognize the way NTFS organizes files. (You can also encounter this situation if you must archive files from systems that do not run Windows NT on a system that runs under Windows NT.)

Under these circumstances, you must maintain the other file system on a separate hard drive or on a separate partition on the same hard drive. Windows NT can recognize these volumes, and automatically converts files that are copied from one partition to another to the appropriate file system. As your needs change, you can always convert a partition to the NT file system by using the CONVERT command at the command prompt.

TIP

To convert a drive partition to NTFS, use the following command from the command prompt:

convert *driveletter* /fs:ntfs

You cannot convert the drive whose letter shows in the command prompt. If Windows NT cannot convert the drive when you issue the command, it converts the next time you boot.

How Many Operating Systems Do I Need on My Computer?

When To Use

With Windows NT, you can have multiple operating systems present on your computer, and you can choose which one to run when your computer boots. This section explains why you might decide to have multiple operating systems on your computer.

Notes

You need access to the operating systems that make your applications work. If you are working only with applications that you know are compatible with Windows NT, Windows NT is the only operating system you need to have installed. You can run your applications and accomplish your work without security concerns that occur by having more than one operating system installed on your computer.

There are two situations for which you may need to have multiple operating systems. The first is because Windows NT does not allow any application program direct access to the hardware in your system. For most applications, this requirement poses no problem. Most operating systems enable programmers to directly manipulate the hardware, however, and to bypass the operating system's control. Programs that attempt to directly manipulate hardware fail under Windows NT because NT refuses to allow such manipulation. When using application programs designed in this fashion, keep the operating system that allows direct hardware manipulation on your system.

The other situation that demands multiple operating systems occurs when you want to maintain both operating systems. Examples of such situations are as follows:

- You are responsible for testing applications to ensure that they can run under Windows NT without modification.

- You are responsible for modifying applications so that they run under Windows NT.

- Your job function requires you to maintain both operating systems. An example is to write company support manuals for users who routinely use Windows for Workgroups, but whose file server runs under Windows NT.

You can always start with multiple operating systems on your computer and eliminate those you no longer need later. Chapter 2 tells you how to do this.

Windows NT Setup

In this chapter, you find descriptions of the procedures for installing and configuring Windows NT. You learn about setting up your system, using and optimizing memory, and managing network connections.

The information is organized into the following tasks:

- Using Setup to install Windows NT

- Using Setup to change hardware

- Using Setup to add or remove Windows components

- Using Setup to add or remove SCSI adapters

- Using Setup to add or remove tape devices

- Using Setup to delete user profiles

- Using the Control Panel to install and remove drivers

- Managing network settings

- Using virtual memory

- Managing tasking

- Selecting the operating system
- Setting environment variables
- Optimizing your computer system
- Monitoring memory usage

Using Setup To Install Windows

When To Use

Use the Windows NT Setup utility to install Windows NT on your system or to make changes in the way Windows NT runs on your system.

Steps To Follow

To install Windows for the first time, follow these steps for an x86-based computer:

1. Turn the computer off.

2. Insert Windows NT Disk #1 into drive A, and insert the CD (if one is included in your package) into the CD-ROM drive.

3. Turn the computer on.

4. Follow the directions that Windows NT Setup provides on-screen to complete the setup process.

If your Windows NT package includes a CD, but your CD-ROM drive is not supported, do the following:

1. Start your computer, and boot MS-DOS.

2. Place the CD in the CD-ROM drive, and place a blank high-density floppy disk, formatted under MS-DOS, in your boot drive.

3. Change to your CD-ROM drive.

4. Change to the \i386 directory.

5. Enter the following command, and press Enter:

    `WINNT`

6. Follow the directions on the screen.

To install Windows NT on a RISC-based computer for the first time, follow these steps:

1. Place the Windows NT compact disc into your CD-ROM drive.

2. Run the program named Setupldr, which is in the \MIPS directory.

3. Follow the directions that Windows NT Setup provides on-screen to complete the setup process.

Notes

If you are installing Windows NT on a computer that has an operating system and applications installed on it, back up the hard drive before attempting installation.

Windows NT Setup may need to format your hard disk for several reasons. You may not have enough space to store Windows NT files during the setup process (approximately 70M). You may choose to use a file system that is different from the one previously installed on the drive. Or, you may choose to repartition all or part of your drive so that Windows NT and another operating system can coexist on your drive.

In any case, it is possible to become confused during setup and authorize the setup program to inadvertently format all or part of your drive. Having a backup of your data is both cheap and wise protection against such confusion.

If you have a device (monitor, mouse, or other peripheral) that is packaged with a custom device driver, you can install the device driver when you run Setup for the first time. Select the Custom Setup option, and change the default options after the list of hardware options appears. The Setup utility prompts you to insert the disk with the custom device driver.

Windows NT includes Express and Custom setup options. The Express option automatically detects your hardware configuration, and installs the correct drivers and components.

Custom setup requires that you designate hardware configuration by selecting options from drop-down list boxes. You need to use Custom setup only if you are using hardware that is not explicitly named on the Windows NT hardware-compatibility list.

After the initial installation, you can run Windows NT Setup from within Windows NT to change the configuration of the operating system.

When you install Windows NT, you must establish a user account for the system administrator who must enter a password at the time of installation. The administrator's password needs to be kept secure, but it also needs to be remembered. If the administrator forgets the password, the only option is to reinstall Windows NT.

Setup installs the following files on your hard drive. You should never delete these files, especially while using another operating system. These files are required to start Windows NT.

The following files are on the C drive of an x86 system in the root directory:

AUTOEXEC.NT

BOOT.INI

BOOTSECT.DOS

CONFIG.NT

NTBOOTDD.SYS

NTDETECT.COM

NTLDR

PAGEFILE.SYS

The following files are on the system partition of a RISC system:

AUTOEXEC.NT

CONFIG.NT

HAL.DLL

OSLOADER.EXE

PAGEFILE.SYS

Using Setup To Change Hardware

When To Use

Run Setup from within Windows NT to see what types of hardware drivers are installed and to change installed drivers.

Steps To Follow

1. From the Program Manager window, open the Main group by double-clicking on its icon.

2. Open the Windows NT Setup utility by double-clicking on its icon.

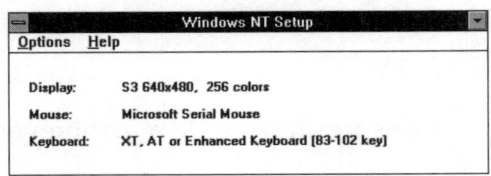

3. Read the current settings, as shown in the Windows NT Setup window.

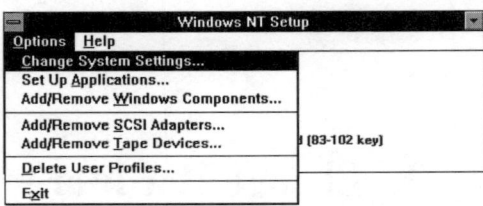

4. To change the installed hardware drivers, select the Options menu from the Windows Setup menu bar, and choose the Change System Settings menu item.

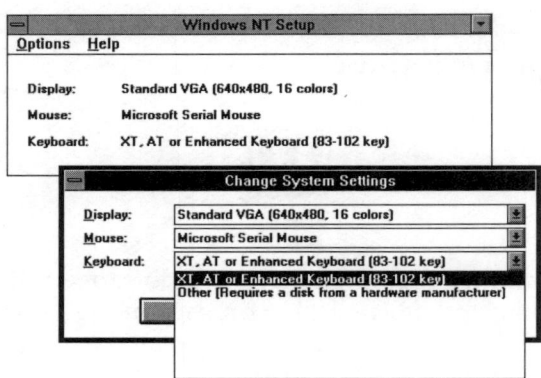

5. Use the drop-down lists to select a new hardware driver. Click on the down arrow, then click on the driver you want.

6. Click on the OK button to accept the changes.

 Windows NT may ask for files locat-
ed on the installation disks or the
CD-ROM, so have them handy. Also,
for some hardware drivers, you may
have to insert appropriate disks into
floppy drives.

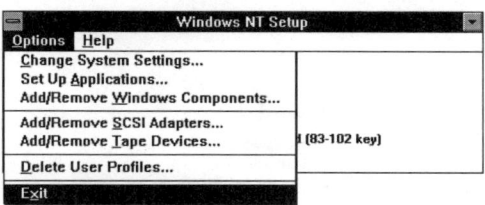

7. Select the Options menu, and choose Exit to end
   Setup.

Notes

To install third-party software (device drivers that do
not appear on the drop-down lists) for a device you
have not previously installed, select Other (Requires
disk from the hardware manufacturer). When
prompted to do so, insert the disk containing the
driver into drive A, and click on the OK button.

The Set Up Applications command in the Options
menu within the Setup window searches the hard disk
drive for Windows applications, POSIX applications,
and DOS applications. This action installs these applications as icons in the Applications group in Program
Manager.

Using Setup To Add or
Remove Windows Components

When To Use

Because Windows NT is such a large software package,
you may not want to have all of it installed all the

time. Use Setup to add programs from the Windows NT package that are not installed, or use it to remove programs from the Windows NT package when you need space on your hard disk.

Steps To Follow

1. From the Program Manager window, open the Main group by double-clicking on its icon.

2. Open the Windows NT Setup utility by double-clicking on its icon.

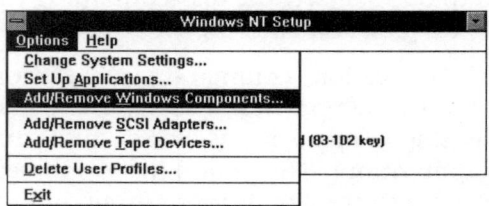

3. To add or remove Windows components, select the Options menu from the Windows Setup menu bar, and choose Add/Remove Windows Components.

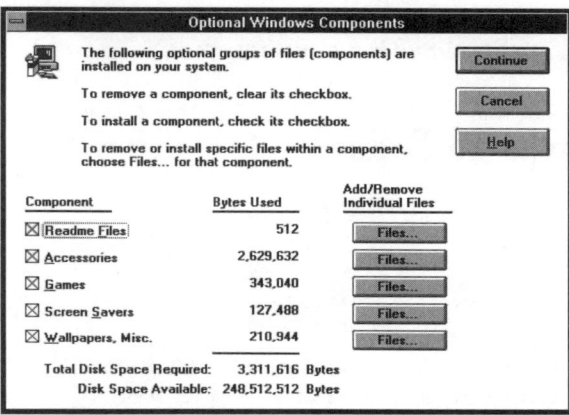

4. To install a component, check its check box by clicking on it with the mouse. To remove a component, uncheck its check box by clicking on it with the mouse.

5. To accept the changes, click on the Continue button, and follow the instructions in the dialog boxes that appear on the screen. To cancel changes, click on the Cancel button.

Notes

The Files button on the right of each check box enables you to select which files are added and removed. Clicking on the Files button presents a list of the files in that group. Double-clicking on a file name moves it between the Do not install and Install list boxes. Click on the OK button to accept the changes.

Using Setup To Add or Remove SCSI Adapters

When To Use

Use Setup to add or remove SCSI adapters when you have installed a new SCSI adapter on your system or removed a SCSI adapter from your system. (SCSI stands for *small computer systems interface*.)

Steps To Follow

1. From the Program Manager window, open the Main group by double-clicking on its icon.

2. Open the Windows NT Setup utility by double-clicking on its icon.

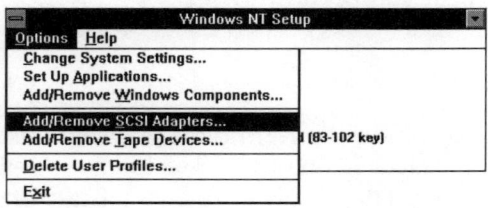

3. Select the Add/Remove SCSI Adapters option from the Options menu.

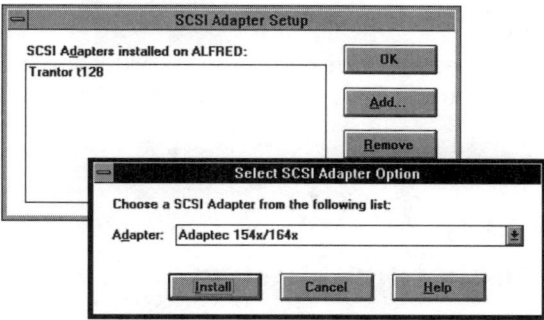

4. Click on the **A**dd button to add an adapter. Select the adapter from the drop-down list box by clicking on the arrow and clicking on the name of the adapter. If your adapter is not listed, select Other (Requires disk from hardware manufacturer) on the list, and insert the disk from the manufacturer when prompted to do so. Click on the Install button to install the driver.

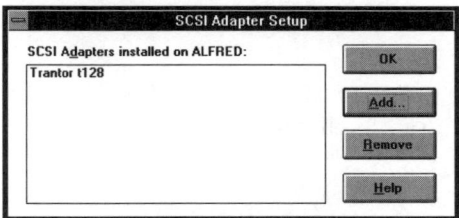

5. To remove an adapter, select it in the list box by clicking on it, and then click on the **R**emove button. Click on the OK button when the dialog box appears to request confirmation.

6. Click on the OK button in the SCSI Adapter Setup dialog box to complete this process.

Notes

You must restart your computer in order for the
changes you made to the SCSI adapter setup to take
effect.

Using Setup To Add
or Remove Tape Devices

When To Use

Use Setup to add or remove tape devices when you
have installed a new tape drive on your system, or if
you have removed a tape drive from your system.

Steps To Follow

1. From the Program Manager window, open the Main
   group by double-clicking on its icon.

2. Open the Windows NT Setup utility by double-
   clicking on its icon.

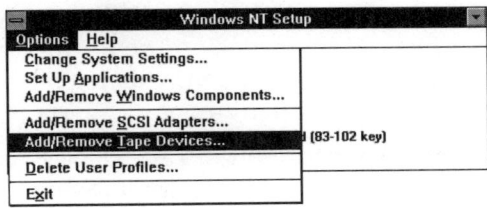

3. Select the Add/Remove Tape Devices option from the Options menu.

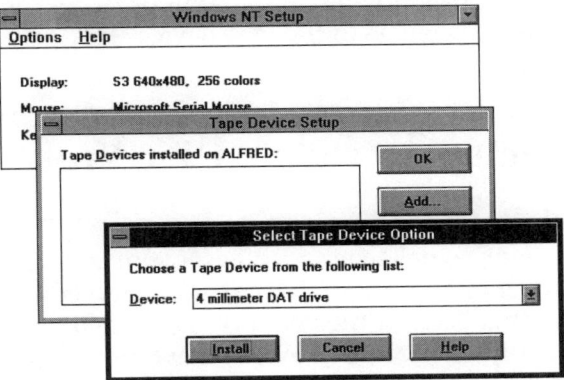

4. Click on the Add button to add an adapter. Select the adapter from the drop-down list box by clicking on the arrow and clicking on the name of the adapter. If your adapter is not listed, select Other (Requires disk from hardware manufacturer) on the list, and insert the disk from the manufacturer when prompted to do so. Click on the Install button to install the driver.

5. To remove an adapter, select it in the list box by clicking on it, and then click on the Remove button. Click on the OK button when the dialog box appears requesting confirmation.

6. Click on the OK button in the Tape Device Setup dialog box to complete adding or removing a Tape Device.

Notes

You must restart your computer in order for the changes you made to the tape device setup to take effect.

Using Setup To Delete User Profiles

When To Use

Use Setup to delete user profiles if your computer is a member of a Windows NT Advanced Server network, and other users of the network log on to the network from your workstation. When other users log on, their user profiles are copied to your workstation. You can delete these extra profiles as necessary to save space and promote security. (The original profile is protected safely in the user's configuration registry.)

Steps To Follow

1. From the Program Manager window, open the Main group by double-clicking on its icon.

2. Open the Windows NT Setup utility by double-clicking on its icon.

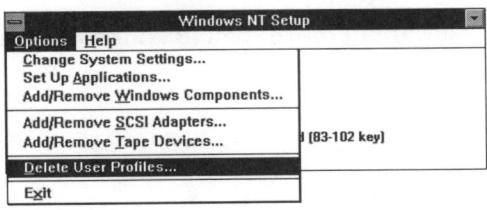

3. Select the <u>D</u>elete User Profiles option on the <u>O</u>ptions menu.

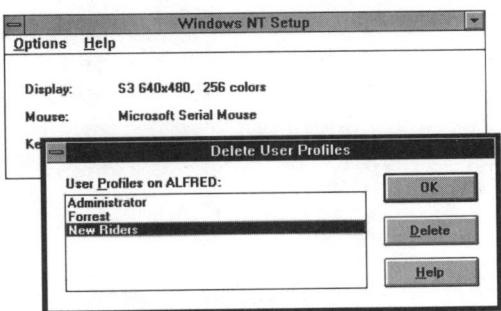

4. Select the user profile from the list box. Click on the <u>D</u>elete button to delete the user profile.

5. Click on the OK button in the Delete User Profile dialog box when you are finished.

Notes

To delete user profiles, you must be logged on with administrative privileges. If you do not have the appropriate privileges, a dialog box tells you so.

Be certain that you want to delete the profile before you do so. No confirmation is required.

 **WARNING** Be careful not to delete your own user profile by accident.

˙ Using Control Panel To Install and Remove Drivers

When To Use

Use the Drivers icon in the Control Panel to install or remove drivers so that Windows NT can control devices such as sound boards and video players.

Steps To Follow

Main

1. From the Program Manager window, open the Main group by double-clicking on its icon.

2. Open the Control Panel by double-clicking on its icon.

3. Open the Drivers dialog box by double-clicking on its icon.

To remove a driver, follow these steps:

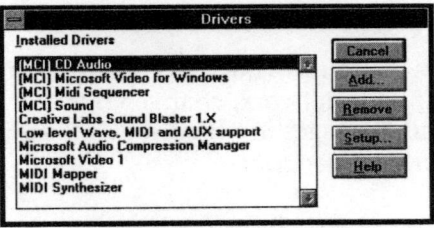

4. Highlight the driver by clicking on it. Click on the Remove button.

5. Click on the Yes button after the warning dialog box appears. (To cancel the operation, click on the No button.)

To add a driver, follow these steps:

4. Click on the Add button.

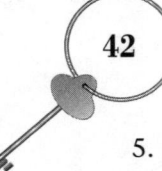

5. Highlight the driver you want to add. Click on the OK button.

6. Place the disk containing the driver in the floppy disk drive after the dialog box prompt appears, then click on the OK button.

Notes

If a driver can be reconfigured, the Setup button becomes active when the driver's name is highlighted in the Drivers dialog box. Clicking on the Setup button activates a dialog box that enables you to change the settings for the driver.

Managing Network Settings

When To Use

While Windows is running, use the Control Panel to log on and off your network, change your user ID or password, send messages to other network users, and restore network connections.

Steps To Follow

1. From the Program Manager window, open the Main group by double-clicking on its icon.

2. Open the Control Panel by double-clicking on its icon.

3. Open the Network Settings dialog box by double-clicking on its icon.

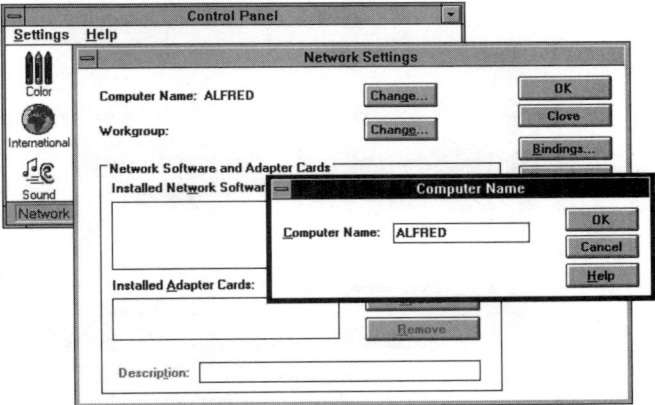

4. Use the Change button to change the name of your computer. Enter the new name in the dialog box and click on OK.

5. Use the Change button to change the Workgroup or Domain to which you are currently joined. In the Domain/Workgroup Settings dialog box, select either Workgroup or Domain by using the option buttons in the Member of: group. Enter the name of the domain or workgroup in the appropriate text box, and click on OK to make the change.

6. To create an account within a domain, check the Create Computer Account in Domain check box after completing step 4. Enter the domain administrator's user name and password in the text boxes, then click on OK.

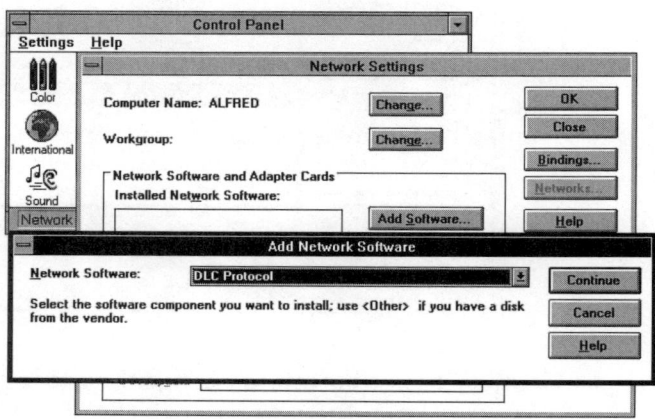

7. Use the Add Software button to install network software components. Select the name of the software component in the drop-down list box, and click on the Continue button. If you select Other (Requires disk from manufacturer) on the list, insert the disk containing the software component in drive A when prompted to do so.

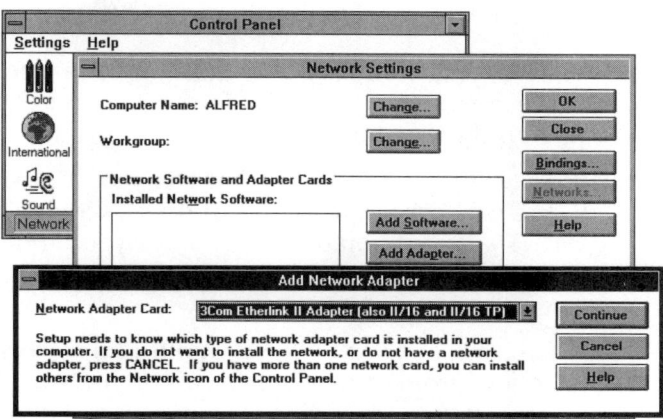

8. Use the Add Adapter button to install network adapter card drivers. Select the name of the network adapter card in the drop-down list box, and click on the Continue button. If you select Other (Requires disk from manufacturer) on the list, insert the disk containing the network adapter card driver in drive A when prompted to do so.

9. Use the Configure button to configure any installed network software component or driver. Select the driver or software component in the appropriate list box, and click on the Configure button. Adjust the settings in the dialog box that appears, and click on OK.

10. Use the Update button to install new versions of existing drivers or software components on your system. Enter the name of the driver in the dialog box that appears.

11. Use the Remove button to remove an installed driver or software component. Select the driver or component in the appropriate list box, and click on the Remove button.

12. Use the Bindings button to adjust the relationships between network drivers and software components. Adjust the settings in the dialog boxes that appear.

Notes

The Network Settings dialog box is much more consistent across networks in Windows NT than in other versions of Windows.

Binding describes the ways that software components in the network relate to one another. Networking software is configured as a series of layers, and each component is *bound* to one or more components in the layers above and below it.

A *domain* is a group of workstations and servers, which is isolated from other domains on the network for several reasons, including security. Several domains can exist on the same network but not have access to each other's files and applications.

A *workgroup* is a set of workstations and servers that are grouped together to enable the sharing of resources. Workgroups are typically not isolated for security reasons. They are most often used to grant privileges to multiple users within a domain.

Using Virtual Memory

When To Use

Windows NT requires a paging file that must be a mimimum of 20M in size. It is similar to the Windows 3.1 swap file. You can use the System icon in the Control Panel to create or change this virtual memory file. (*Virtual memory* is memory on the disk that is treated as if it were a part of the system RAM.)

Steps To Follow

1. From the Program Manager window, open the Main group by double-clicking on its icon.

2. Open the Control Panel by double-clicking on its icon.

3. Open the System dialog box by double-clicking on its icon.

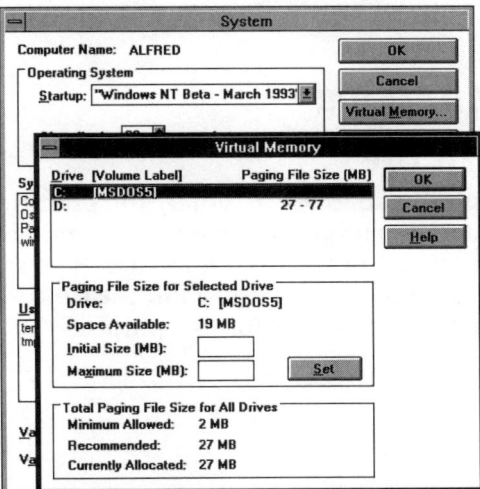

4. Open the Virtual Memory dialog box by clicking on the Virtual Memory button.

5. Select the disk drive on which you want to create or modify the paging file from the Drive list box.

6. Enter the Initial Size and Maximum Size as a number of megabytes in the text boxes.

7. Click on the Set button.

8. Click on the OK button, then click on the Close button.

Notes

You must have administrative privileges in order to adjust the size of the paging file, which is placed as a hidden file called PAGEFILE.SYS on the drive you selected. Windows NT does not allow you to delete this file. If you delete it while using another operating system on your computer, Windows NT automatically creates a new paging file when you start Windows NT again.

You must allocate at least 20M to the paging file. The typical recommended size is the amount of RAM on your system plus 12M. For Windows NT, it is best to use the recommended size.

Managing Tasking

When To Use

Windows NT enables you to adjust the priorities associated with background and foreground tasks so that the response of your system matches your working style. Use the Tasking button in the Control Panel's System dialog box for this purpose.

Steps To Follow

1. From the Program Manager window, open the Main group by double-clicking on its icon.

2. Open the Control Panel by double-clicking on its icon.

3. Open the System dialog box by double-clicking on its icon.

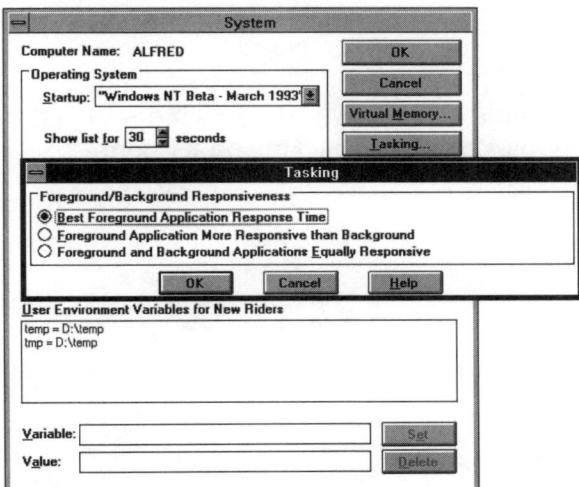

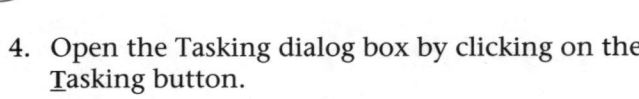

4. Open the Tasking dialog box by clicking on the Tasking button.

5. Select the tasking priorities by using the option buttons to optimize the system for your working style so that applications running in the foreground are as responsive as you want.

6. Click on the OK button in the Tasking dialog box, then click on the OK button in the System dialog box.

Selecting the Operating System

When To Use

Windows NT enables you to keep multiple operating systems on your computer and to choose between them at boot time. The Control Panel's System icon enables you to select the operating system(s) that your computer can use.

Steps To Follow

1. From the Program Manager window, open the Main group by double-clicking on its icon.

2. Open the Control Panel by double-clicking on its icon.

3. Open the System dialog box by double-clicking on its icon.

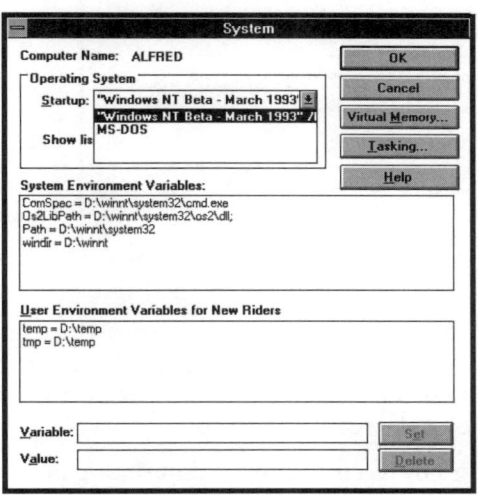

4. Select the operating system you want to start by default by using the $\underline{S}$tartup drop-down list box in the Operating System group. Click on the arrow, then click on the name of the operating system.

   Flex boot, the program that enables you to choose the operating system, starts this operating system by default if you do not choose one from the list it presents.

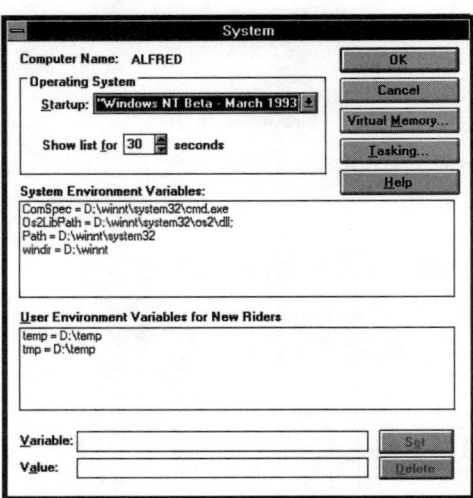

5. Choose the amount of waiting time for selecting an operating system from flex boot's list in the Show list for text box. Click on the arrow buttons to increase or decrease the time.

6. Click on OK to close the System dialog box.

Notes

If you have another operating system on your computer when you install Windows NT, Setup automatically installs flex boot so that you can run multiple operating systems.

Flex boot is a program that presents a list of operating systems for you to choose from when your computer starts. After a default waiting period of 30 seconds, flex boot starts the first operating system on the list if you do not make a selection.

Windows NT can support multiple operating systems, but it can support only one alternate *root-based operating system*, which requires that certain files be present in the root directory of your boot drive. MS-DOS and OS/2 are root-based operating systems.

To temporarily disable the multiple-boot feature of your computer, clear the <u>S</u>tartup drop-down list box in the System dialog box. This action causes Windows NT to boot immediately when you start the system.

To remove MS-DOS (or another operating system) permanently from your computer, disable the multiple-boot feature. Then take the following three steps:

1. Delete all MS-DOS files.

2. Copy CONFIG.NT and AUTOEXEC.NT to CONFIG.SYS and AUTOEXEC.BAT.

3. Run CONVERT.EXE to convert all FAT partitions to the NT File System if you want to take advantage of NTFS and security features. Remember that you are not required to convert to NTFS, and that the conversion is one way.

Setting Environment Variables

When To Use

Set environment variables to tell Windows NT where to find temporary directories, drives, and applications. An important environment variable is PATH, which functions like the MS-DOS PATH variable.

Steps To Follow

1. From the Program Manager window, open the Main group by double-clicking on its icon.

2. Open the Control Panel by double-clicking on its icon.

3. Open the System dialog box by double-clicking on its icon.

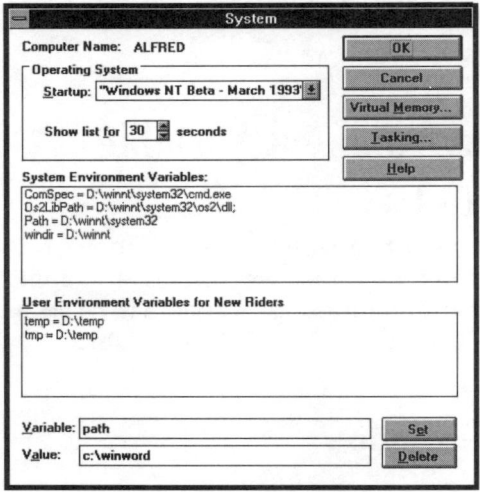

4. Enter the name of the variable in the Variable text box.

5. Enter the value of the variable in the Value text box.

6. Click on the Set button.

7. Click on OK to close the System dialog box.

Notes

You can change the value for an existing environment variable by clicking on its name in the User Environment Variables for list box, entering the new value in the Value text box, and clicking on the Set button.

Optimizing Your Computer System

When To Use

In Windows 3.1, there are a number of tricks that you can perform on your system to optimize its performance. In Windows NT, however, optimizations are performed for you automatically—you no longer need to adjust settings in the WIN.INI files and SYSTEM.INI files to get the best performance out of your system.

Notes

All optimizations for Windows NT are performed by a part of the operating system known as the *hardware abstraction layer*. Although there is a file in the \WINNT\SYSTEM32 directory (HAL.DLL) that contains these optimizations, you cannot alter it or adjust it.

You also find WIN.INI and SYSTEM.INI in the \WINNT\SYSTEM directory, but these are for compatibility with Windows 3.1 applications only. You should not have to modify these files at all.

Monitoring Memory Usage

When To Use

Check the system memory if you have questions about the amount of memory available to applications.

Steps To Follow

1. Select the Help menu in any Windows application, and choose the About option.

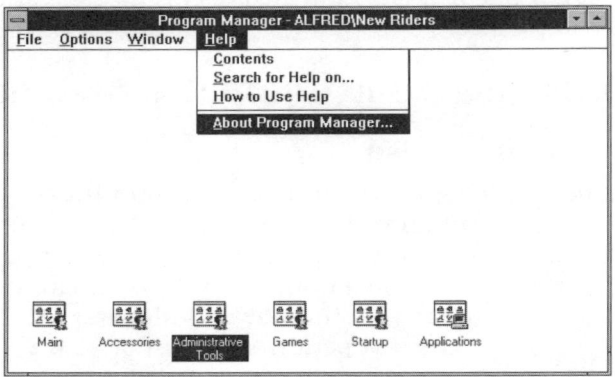

2. Note the amount of physical memory reported.

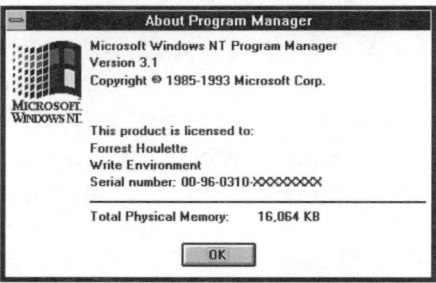

3. Click on the OK button to clear the dialog box from the screen.

Notes

The About dialog boxes for Program Manager, File Manager, and the accessories that come with Windows report the total physical memory available. The About boxes for most Windows programs also report this information. If you do not find the About box in your current application, switch to an application that shipped with your Windows package and check there.

Applications that are written for Windows 3.1 often report a slightly larger amount of available physical memory than applications written for Windows NT do. The discrepancies in the report have to do with the way Windows NT answers the query issued by the application about available memory. Queries from applications written for NT are answered with a report of physical memory size. Queries from applications written for 16-bit Windows include additional memory resources that are relevant to the application.

Log-on and Administrative Tasks

Windows NT is different from Windows 3.1 in that it requires you to follow certain security procedures. Although these procedures are simple and straightforward, you have to think differently about your system—you cannot just flip the power switch on and wait for the machine to boot anymore. Once Windows NT has booted, you are locked out of the system until you log on. You must learn new habits in order to use your system effectively and protect your data. This chapter describes these essential habits.

The information is organized into the following tasks:

- Logging on
- Logging off
- Locking your workstation
- Shutting the system down
- Setting up user accounts

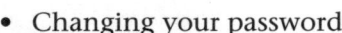

- Changing your password
- Monitoring your system for security problems
- Disabling an account
- Forcing a user to change passwords

Logging On
When To Use

Windows NT requires that you log on to your system by using a password to gain access to your applications and data. Follow this procedure to gain access to your system.

Steps To Follow

1. At the initial log-on screen, press Ctrl-Alt-Delete.

2. When the Welcome dialog box appears, enter your user name in the **U**sername text box, the domain or computer name in the **F**rom text box, and your password in the **P**assword text box.

3. Click on the OK button. If Windows NT can match your user name and password to its database of user names, it admits you to the system.

Notes

When logging on to a computer running Windows NT, always press Ctrl-Alt-Delete. Pressing this key sequence is an important security procedure. This procedure guarantees that you are entering your user name and password in the Welcome dialog box displayed by Windows NT. Someone could write a program that displays a look-alike screen in order to steal user names and passwords. One of your best lines of defense against unauthorized use of your system is pressing Ctrl-Alt-Delete.

 You should report any unusual log-on events to your system administrator, especially if the system reboots mysteriously or takes an unusually long time to admit you.

Under Windows NT, each computer or group of networked computers (*domain*) has a name. You need to identify your computer or domain by name at the time you log on. These names contain up to 15 characters, without spaces or punctuation.

Windows NT requires you to use a password to access your system. Your password may be up to 20 characters in length, with no spaces or punctuation. Good passwords are memorable but not guessable.

 You can make a very secure password by running several words together, for example, BlowTheDuckOver. You should change your password frequently, and if you write it down, keep it locked up.

If you are the administrator of your system, you may be tempted to create a user name without a password in order to simplify the log-on process. You also might want to give this user account administrator privileges, in case the system refuses to recognize your administrator's password.

Creating such a user account is extremely unwise. If anyone should discover it, he can get immediate access to the system, your applications, and your data. If you have given the account administrator privileges, the person who has gained access unscrupulously can do anything to the system he likes, including destroying data.

Logging Off

When To Use

When you are finished using your computer, but you do not want to shut it down, you should log off the computer so that no one can gain unauthorized access to the system.

Steps To Follow

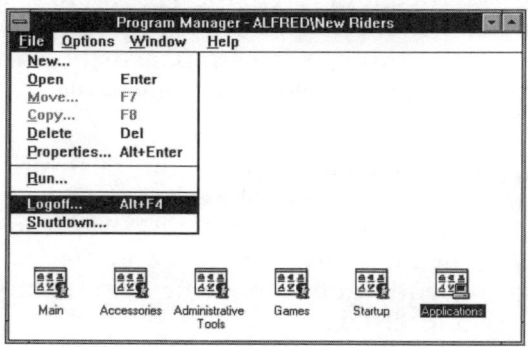

1. Make Program Manager the active application, and click on its **F**ile menu.

2. Choose the **L**ogoff menu option.

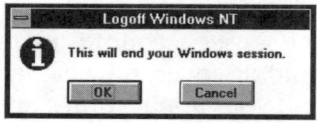

3. Click on the OK button in the Logoff Windows NT dialog box. Windows NT closes your user account and returns you to the welcome screen.

Notes

You should always log off the system when you will not be using it for extended periods of time. Logging off provides the greatest security protection.

Screen savers also make use of passwords in Windows NT, and they provide a certain level of security. Because they are popular third-party programs, however, you should not rely on them excessively. Someone can write a screen saver that attempts to steal passwords.

You can also log off the system by pressing Ctrl-Alt-Delete to bring up the Windows NT Security dialog box, and then click on the **L**ogoff button.

Locking Your Workstation

When To Use

Lock your workstation whenever you leave it for a short time and do not want to log off.

Steps To Follow

1. Press Ctrl-Alt-Delete while you are logged on to your system.

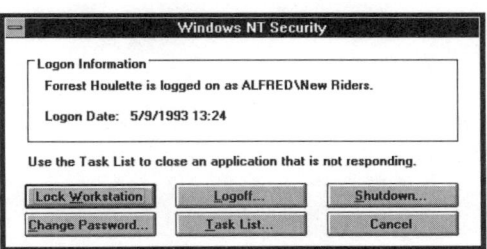

2. In the Windows NT Security dialog box, click on the Lock **W**orkstation button.

3. Windows NT displays the Workstation Is Locked
    dialog box on your screen.

Notes

Screen savers automatically lock your workstation
when you enable the password option for the screen
saver in the Control Panel.

See Chapter 5 for more information
about using screen savers.

Be immediately suspicious if a screen saver prompts
you to enter a password when you come back to work.
You should see a Windows NT dialog box, which
announces that the workstation is locked and tells you
who has locked it. Windows NT requires you to press
Ctrl-Alt-Delete before it prompts you for a password.

Shutting the System Down

When To Use

When you want to power down your computer, use
Windows NT's shutdown procedure to exit the operating system.

Steps To Follow

1. Make Program Manager the active application, and
    click on the File menu.

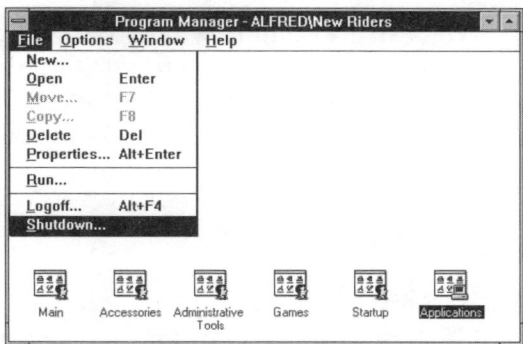

2. Select the **S**hutdown menu option.

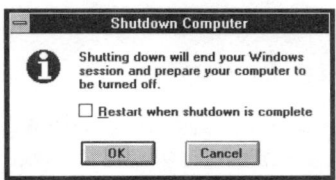

3. Click on the OK button in the Shutdown Computer dialog box.

4. Do not turn your computer off until the Shutdown Computer dialog box appears again, telling you that it is safe to do so.

Notes

Always use the shutdown procedure before turning your computer off. If you do not, running programs and operating-system services cannot exit properly and save their data. You can lose operating-system data, or your files can be corrupted if you do not use the shutdown procedure.

If you need to shut down in order to reboot, check the **R**estart when shutdown is complete check box in the Shutdown Computer dialog box (see step 2).

NOTE You can also shut down the system by pressing Ctrl-Alt-Delete to bring up the Windows NT Security dialog box, and click on the **S**hutdown button.

Setting Up User Accounts

When To Use

You should set up a user account for each person who will use your system. Thus, you restrict the persons who use your computer, and you control how they can use your computer.

Steps To Follow

1. Log on to your system as the Administrator. If you do not administer your system, choose a user name that is a member of the Power Users group.

2. In Program Manager, open the Administrative Tools group by double-clicking on its icon.

3. Open the User Manager application by double-clicking on its icon.

4. Click on the **U**ser menu, and select the New **U**ser option.

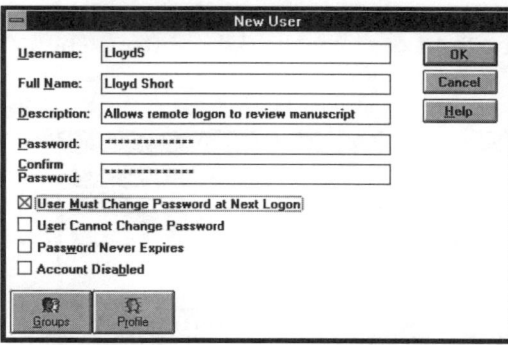

5. In the New User dialog box, enter a unique user name (with a maximum length of twenty characters) in the **U**sername text box.

6. Enter the user's full name in the Full **N**ame text box. (This record enables you to associate a real name with sometimes cryptic user names.)

7. Enter a description of the account (describing the account's intended use) in the **D**escription text box.

8. Enter a password in both the **P**assword and **C**onfirm Password text boxes.

9. Check the following check boxes, if appropriate: User **M**ust Change Password at Next Logon, the U**s**er Cannot Change Password, and the Pass**w**ord Never Expires.

10. Click on the **G**roups button to open the Group Memberships dialog box.

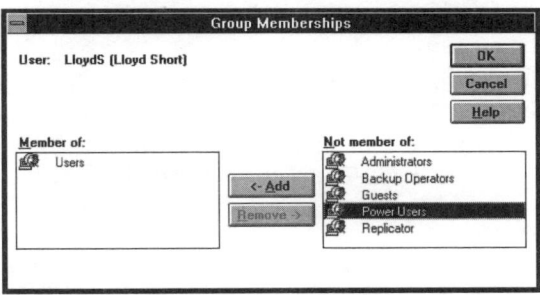

11. Highlight the groups to which the user should belong, and click on the **A**dd button. Then click on the OK button.

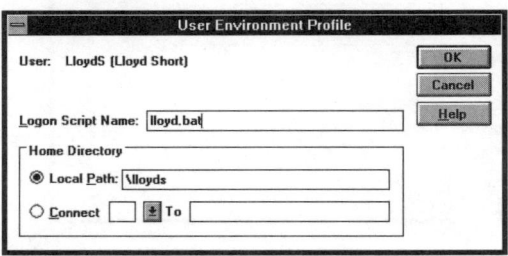

12. Click on the P**r**ofile button in the New User dialog box to open the User Environment Profile dialog box.

13. Enter a log-on script name if you want a file of commands to execute at the time the user logs on to the system. (*Log-on scripts* are like AUTOEXEC.BAT files for Windows NT.) Do not include a path—just enter the script name.

14. In the Home Directory group, select one of the options if you want the user to have a home directory (the default directory) in which to work.

A *home directory* is like a working directory that you can set for an application program in Program Manager. In fact, you can probably set up most applications to store the user's data files in her home directory.

15. You can enter a directory on the local hard drive in the Local **P**ath text box, or you can select a **D**rive on the network, and specify a directory on that drive in the To text box. Then click on the OK button.

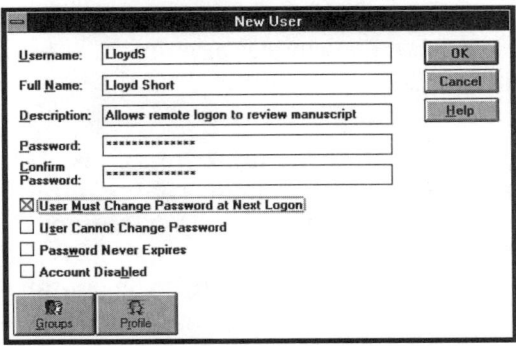

16. Click on the OK button in the New User dialog box.

Notes

You must be logged on as Administrator or as a member of the Power Users group to create new user accounts. Only Administrators and Power Users can create new accounts.

A *user account* is a collection of information about each user. It contains the information that you enter in the New User dialog box, plus all of the system settings that the user has chosen for using and customizing Windows NT.

A *group* is a group of users who all share the same privileges on the system. For example, members of the Users group can run most applications and make effective use of the system. Members of the Backup Operators group have additional privileges that allow them to make backups of drives, but they are not allowed full control of the system. Members of the Power Users group can create new user accounts, but they do not have full control of the system as members of the Administrator's group do.

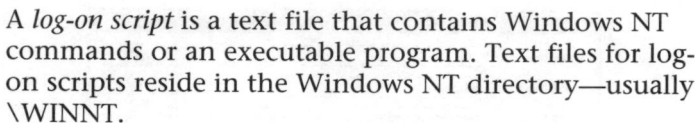

A *log-on script* is a text file that contains Windows NT commands or an executable program. Text files for log-on scripts reside in the Windows NT directory—usually \WINNT.

Windows NT runs the log-on script as the last step in logging a user on to the system. The script can be a text file that has the BAT or CMD extension. If so, each of the Windows NT commands in the file is run exactly as if the user typed them at the command prompt.

If the script is an executable program, Windows NT runs that program. Log-on scripts can be used to set up a user's environment the way an AUTOEXEC.BAT file does under DOS, or they can be used to limit a user's access to system resources. If you want a user to have access to only one application, for instance, you can run it by using the log-on script.

Anyone can use your system by logging on using the user name guest. The guest account has very few privileges, but it gives someone the opportunity to use publicly available software to accomplish a quick task.

Changing Your Password

When To Use

You should change your password frequently to protect security on your system. Use this procedure every four to six weeks.

Steps To Follow

1. Press Ctrl-Alt-Delete while you are logged on to your computer.

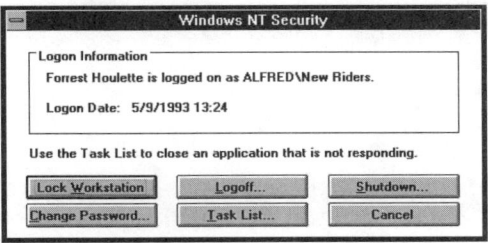

2. Click on the **C**hange Password button when the Windows NT Security dialog box appears.

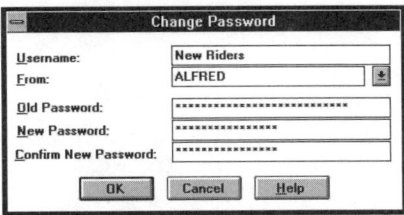

3. In the Change Password dialog box, enter your old password in the **O**ld Password text box.

4. Enter your new password in the **N**ew Password text box.

5. Enter your new password again in the **C**onfirm New Password text box.

6. Click on the OK button.

Notes

On secure systems, you need to change your password frequently. Someone can observe you typing your password at the keyboard, for example, and use the password observed to gain unauthorized access to your user account. To minimize such possibilities, change your password every month or so. Even if someone has acquired it unscrupulously, she will not have many opportunities to cause damage or steal information.

Monitoring Your System for Security Problems

When To Use

Follow this procedure periodically to make sure that no unusual events that indicate security problems are occurring on your system. How frequently you perform this procedure depends on how secure you want your system to be. (If you are not a member of the Administrators group, you cannot perform this procedure effectively.)

Steps To Follow

1. Log on to your system as the Administrator or as a member of the Administrators group.

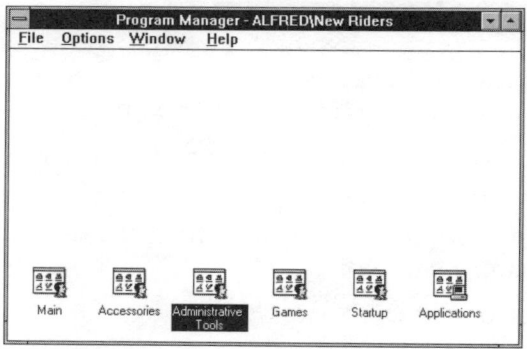

2. In Program Manager, open the Administrative Tools group by double-clicking on its icon.

3. Start the Event Viewer application by double-clicking on its icon.

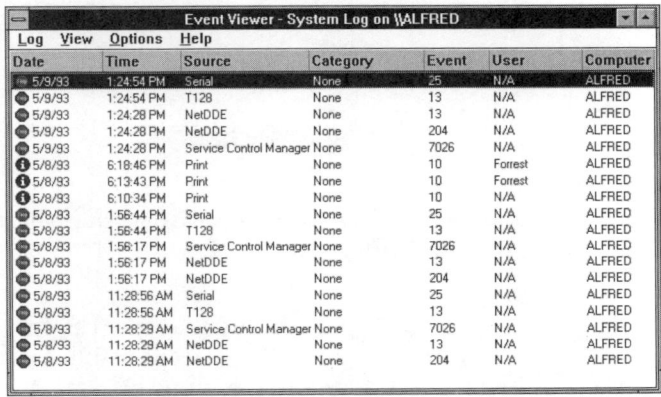

4. Scan the events displayed in the workspace of the application. Look for anything unusual. You may not know what all the events are, but after awhile you will get used to patterns. Unusual patterns can indicate problems.

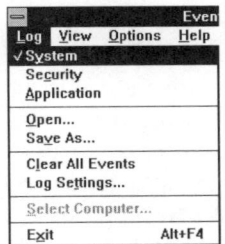

5. Use the options on the **L**og menu to adjust your view of the log. You can view S**y**stem, Se**c**urity, and **A**pplication events. Pay particular attention to the security events.

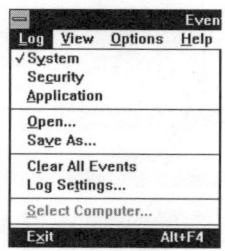

6. Click on E**x**it when you are satisfied that there are no problems indicated.

WARNING If you suspect problems, report them immediately to those responsible for computer security in your organization. If you are responsible for security on your system, see the "Disabling an Account" and "Forcing a User to Change Passwords" sections in this chapter.

Notes

The security log shows all events on the system (failed log-ons, for example) that may indicate that someone is trying to gain unauthorized access. You should pay special attention to security events, and make sure that you understand why each event appears in the log. Users often fail to type passwords correctly, for instance, but repeated failed log-ons over a short period of time may indicate that someone is trying password after password to break in.

Disabling an Account

When To Use

If there is a potential security problem on a system you administer, you should disable the account that represents the problem. If an employee has left your company (or if a user has stopped using your computer), you should disable that account as soon as possible.

Steps To Follow

1. Log on to the system as Administrator or as a member of the Power Users group.

2. In Program Manager, open the Administrative Tools group by double-clicking on its icon.

3. Open the User Manager application by double-clicking on its icon.

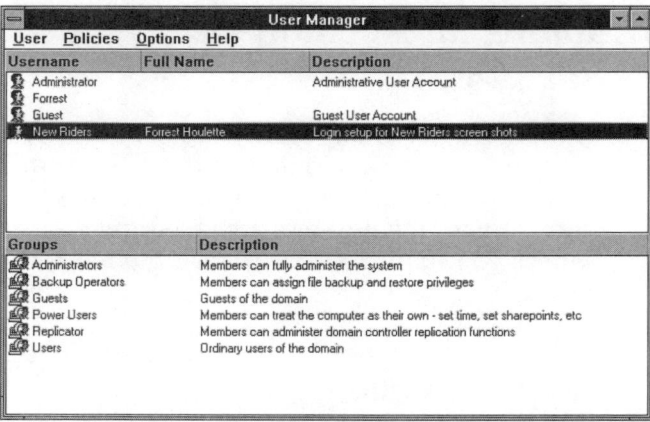

4. Double-click on the name of the user account in the Username section of the workspace.

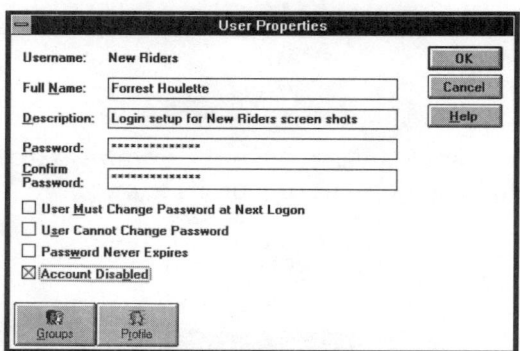

5. In the User Properties dialog box, check Account Disabled.

6. Click on the OK button.

Notes

Disabling an account prevents anyone from logging on to it. If the account is an active one, and you need to have access to it, you can copy it to a new user name

by using the **C**opy option on the **U**ser menu before
disabling it. The user can continue to work under the
new user name, and you have prevented a security
problem.

WARNING   Make sure that the user is not the
security problem before you give him
access to the new copy of the account.

Always disable an account instead of deleting it. You
can clean up the files owned by that user name more
effectively from a disabled account than you can from
a deleted account. Once you have assigned the data
files owned by the user name to other users, you can
delete the account easily by using the **D**elete option on
the **U**ser menu.

To enable an account, repeat this procedure, and clear
the Account Disa**b**led check box.

Forcing a User To Change Passwords

When To Use

If you suspect that a user has been using the same
password for too long, or if you suspect that someone
is trying to break in to an account by guessing the
password, force the user to change passwords.

Steps To Follow

1. Log on to the system as Administrator or as a
   member of the Power Users group.

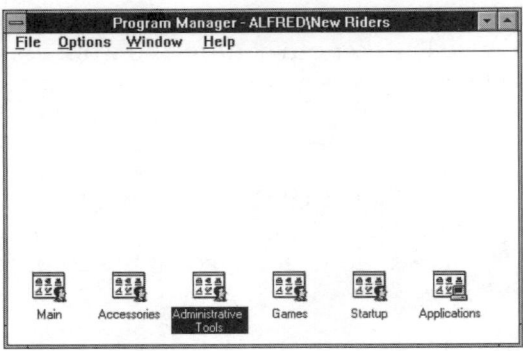

2. In Program Manager, open the Administrative Tools group by double-clicking on its icon.

3. Open the User Manager application by double-clicking on its icon.

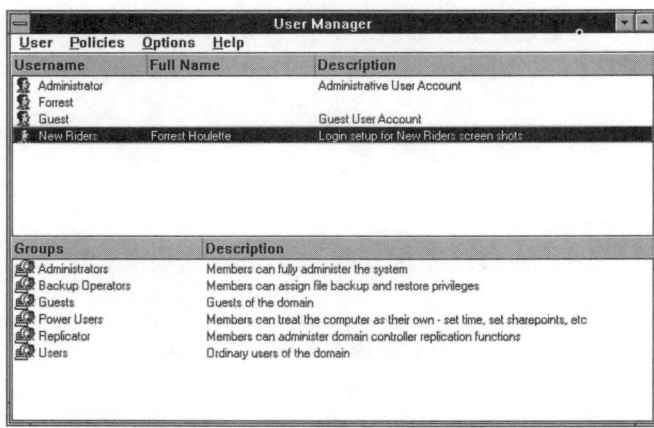

4. Double-click on the name of the user account in the Username section of the workspace.

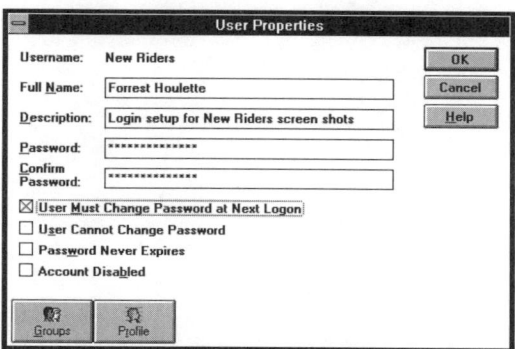

5. In the User Properties dialog box, check User **M**ust Change Password at Next Logon.

6. Click on the OK button.

Notes

After you perform this procedure, Windows NT forces the user to change passwords, as the first step after log-on, the next time the user logs on.

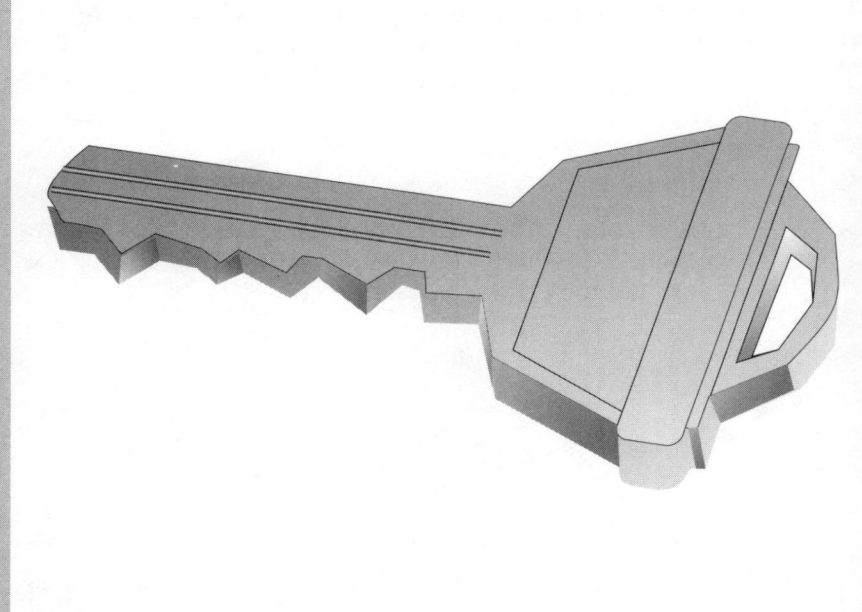

Part Two:
Learning Windows NT Basics

Windows NT Basics

Customizing Windows NT

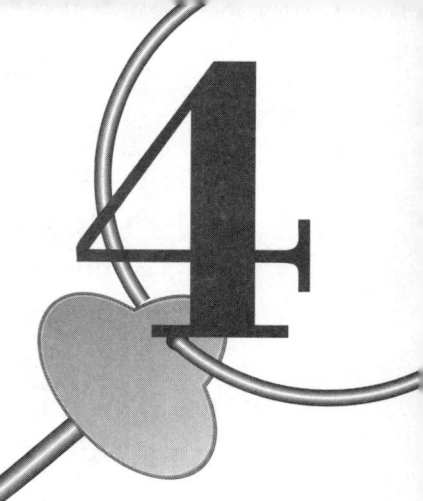

Windows NT Basics

This chapter provides a quick and thorough discussion of the fundamentals of Windows NT. It gives you the skills you need to quickly master Windows NT, which makes you more productive with any Windows NT-compatible application—even those with which you are unfamiliar.

The information is organized into the following tasks:

- Using the Windows NT tutorial
- Comparing your screen to a desktop
- Understanding the application window
- Understanding the document window
- Comparing icon types
- Comparing mouse-pointer types
- Understanding the Control menu
- Arranging the desktop
- Arranging multiple document windows

- Navigating within Windows NT
- Learning common keystrokes
- Mastering common mouse operations
- Learning common Windows NT controls

Using the Windows NT Tutorial

When To Use

Run the Windows NT tutorial to learn about the way
Windows NT operates and how you interact with it.

Steps To Follow

1. In the Program Manager, open the Main group by
   double-clicking on its icon.

2. Start Introducing Windows NT by double-clicking
   on its icon.

3. After the tutorial starts, follow the on-screen directions.

Notes

Introducing Windows NT provides several paths. Each
path constitutes a lesson on a single aspect of using

Windows NT. You can choose from the following lessons by clicking on the button presented by the tutorial:

- **L**ogging on to Windows NT
- **C**onnecting to Other Computers
- **S**haring Files on a Network
- Creating **U**ser Accounts
- Setting File **P**ermissions
- C**o**nnecting to a Printer
- Using Clipbook over the **N**etwork
- Co**m**municating with Other Users

You can, of course, take each lesson sequentially if you want to learn about Windows NT all at once.

 Because Introducing Windows NT is not a Windows program, you may notice some jumpy mouse movements while you are using it. The program also freezes when you shift from full-screen to windowed mode using Alt-Enter. To take the tutorial, you must work in full-screen mode.

Comparing Your Screen to a Desktop
When To Use

Read this section to learn how Windows NT is organized (with a desktop metaphor).

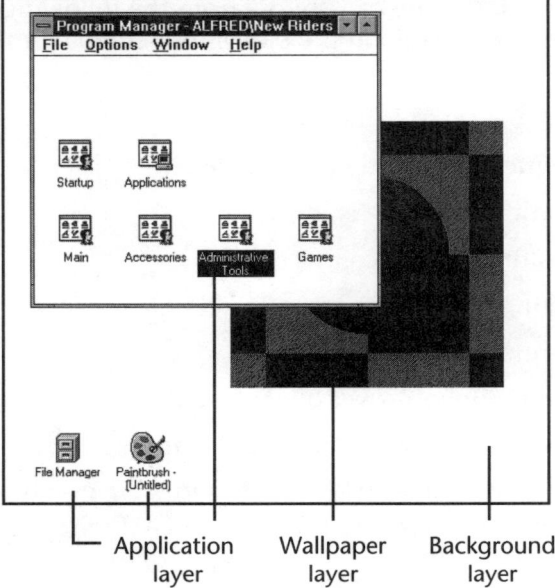

Application   Wallpaper   Background
layer   layer   layer

Notes

Windows NT acts as if your computer screen is the flat surface of a desktop. The application programs are similar to the tools you may have on your desk. The Cardfile program can serve as your Rolodex, for instance, and the Schedule+ program can be your appointment book. Just as you can have several tools laid out on your desk, you also can have several different programs running on the Windows NT desktop.

Windows NT divides the desktop into the following:

• **Background layer**. Represents the surface on which the other two layers rest. In the default Windows NT setup, the background layer appears as a light green. You can, however, change the background color and pattern to suit your preferences (see Chapter 5). Typically, you do not interact with this layer much. If you double-click on this layer, however, the Task List window appears. The Task List gives you control over the other programs running on the desktop.

- **Wallpaper layer.** Holds a picture created by a paint program, and is located on top of the background layer. If the wallpaper is large enough, it completely covers the pattern on the screen (see Chapter 5). Usually, your only interaction with this layer is to change the wallpaper.

- **Application layer.** Contains the windows and icons that represent the programs that are running on your system. This is the desktop layer with which you normally interact as you work. The application layer contains application windows, document windows, and icons.

The *mouse pointer* appears most often as an arrow that is superimposed over the layers of the desktop. It indicates the point on the screen at which the next mouse action will take place. The tip of the arrow is the pointer's hot spot. Make sure that it is over the point at which you want to make a mouse action.

The mouse pointer can take other shapes to tell you more about your system's functions. If a long operation is running, the mouse pointer becomes an hourglass to tell you to wait for the operation to finish before you can continue. If an application is loading but you can continue to work with other applications, the mouse pointer becomes an arrow with the hourglass attached to the right of its stem. If it is over an editable workspace, the mouse pointer becomes the I-beam selection cursor that tells you that you can edit with the mouse.

Understanding the Application Window

When To Use

Read this section to learn about each part and function of an application window.

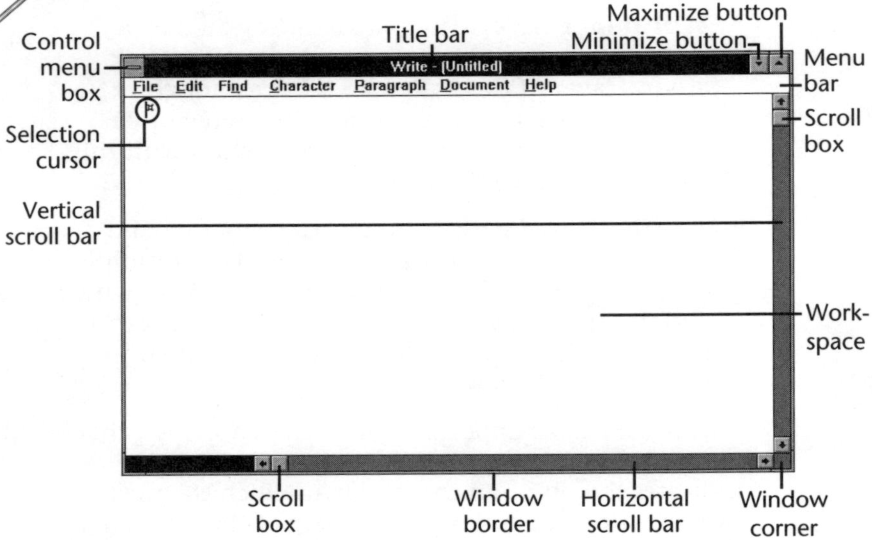

Control menu box — Title bar — Maximize button — Minimize button — Menu bar — Scroll box — Selection cursor — Vertical scroll bar — Work-space — Scroll box — Window border — Horizontal scroll bar — Window corner

Write - [Untitled]

File Edit Find Character Paragraph Document Help

Notes

Application windows contain the applications that run on your system. An application window has several parts, each with its own function (each application window may not have all the components listed). In Windows NT, the components appear as they are needed by the application. Application-window components are as follows:

- **Control menu box.** Discussed later in this chapter.

- **Menu bar.** Presents the application's selection of commands and functions. To display a menu, click on its name on the menu bar. To select a *menu item*, click on it with the mouse. Either the action named by the menu item takes place, or a *cascading menu* drops down to present a list of additional menu items.

The menu bar is organized so that the **F**ile menu is always first on the left (assuming that the application enables file operations). The next menu is the **E**dit menu, if editing functions are

allowed. The menu item on the far
right is always the **H**elp menu, if on-
line help is provided. If the application
makes use of document windows, the
Window menu is immediately to the
left of **H**elp. Any other menu items
provided by the application lie between
Edit and **H**elp on the menu bar.

- **Title bar**. Displays the name of the application. If a
  document completely fills the workspace, the title
  bar also displays the name of the file associated with
  the document. To move the window around on the
  desktop, place the mouse pointer on the title bar,
  and hold the mouse button down as you move the
  mouse. Double-click on the title bar; the window is
  maximized. Double-click again; the window returns
  to its original size.

- **Minimize button**. Shrinks the window to an icon
  after you click on it. The application's icon is returned to the bottom left of the screen. If the icon
  was moved to another desktop location before it was
  executed, its minimized icon returns to that same
  desktop location.

- **Maximize button**. Expands the window to full-
  screen size. If the window is maximized, this button
  changes to a double arrow. Click on the double
  arrow to return the window to its previous size,
  shape, and position.

- **Workspace**. Includes the area of the application
  window in which you work. If the application is a
  word processor, for example, you type and edit text
  in this area.

- **Vertical scroll bars**. Indicate that additional information items exist that are not displayed within
  the vertical area of the workspace. You can scroll the
  workspace up or down to see this information. Click
  on the arrows at the end of the scroll bar to scroll
  the window, one line at a time. (Hold the mouse

button down to repeat scrolling, one line at a time.) Click on the gray area to move the equivalent of one window at a time. (Hold the mouse button down to repeat scrolling, one window at a time.) Drag the scroll box up or down to quickly reposition the information displayed in the workspace.

- **Horizontal scroll bars**. Indicate that additional information items exist that are not displayed within the horizontal area of the workspace. You can scroll the workspace right or left to see this information. Click on the arrows at the end of the scroll bar to scroll the window, one column at a time. (Hold the mouse button down to repeat scrolling, one column at a time.) Click on the gray area to move the equivalent of one window at a time. (Hold the mouse button down to repeat scrolling, one window at a time.) Drag the scroll box left or right to quickly reposition the information in the workspace.

- **Scroll boxes**. Act as dragging points for scrolling, several lines at a time. The scroll box always indicates your relative position in the file by its relative position on the scroll bar.

- **Window border**. The boundary of the application window. If the mouse pointer is over the window border, it becomes a double arrow, indicating that you can resize the window. Drag the border with the mouse to change the dimensions of the application window. Drag the vertical border to change the horizontal dimension. Drag the horizontal border to change the vertical dimension.

- **Window corner**. A special section of the window border. You can change both the horizontal and vertical dimensions of the window at the same time by dragging the window corner.

- **Selection cursor**. Indicates that the mouse can be used to perform editing operations. It is shaped like an I-beam. The mouse pointer becomes the selection cursor whenever it is over an editable workspace.

Understanding the Document Window

When To Use

Read this section to learn the parts of a document window and what they do.

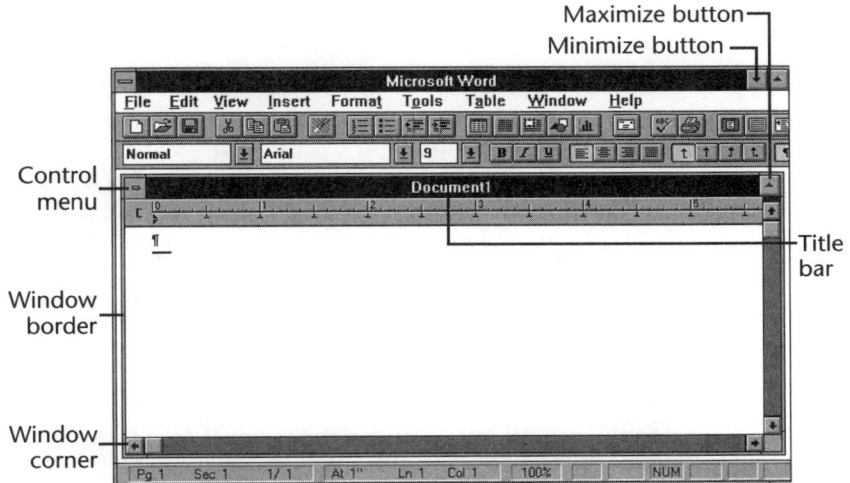

Notes

An application window uses *document windows* to present several different workspaces, each containing a *document*, which is the information processed by the application. In a word processor, the term *document* makes the most sense because each document window presents a document (or file) that is created and saved with the word processor. Each spreadsheet document window presents a different sheet. A document window in Program Manager presents a program group.

Document windows always appear within the workspace of an application window. They may slide under the edge of the application window's border, but the area past the border remains hidden.

Although document windows contain many of the same parts as application windows, some of the parts behave differently. The following lists these differences:

- **Control menu**. Has the same options as the application window, but also has the Nex**t** option. Selecting Nex**t** passes the focus to the next document window on the list that is maintained by the application window.

- **Title bar**. Displays the name of the file presented in that window. Double-click on the title bar to expand the document window to fill the workspace of the application window. The document window's title bar then slides under the application window's menu bar. The application window's title bar displays the name of the file represented by the maximized document window. The document window's Control menu appears at the left edge of the application window's menu bar. The document window's maximize button appears at the right edge of the application window's menu bar.

- **Minimize button**. Shrinks the document window to an icon that appears at the bottom of the application window's workspace. Within applications, the minimize button shrinks a document to an icon that stays inside that application's windows. The icon is not returned to the desktop.

- **Maximize button**. Expands the document window to fill the workspace of the application window. The document window's title bar then slides under the application window's menu bar. The application window's title bar displays the name of the file represented by the maximized document window. The document window's Control menu appears at the left edge of the application window's menu bar. The document window's maximize button appears at the right edge of the application window's menu bar. If the document window is maximized, the maximize button changes to a double arrow. Click on the double arrow to return the document window to its previous size, shape, and position.

- **Window border**. The boundary of the document window. Although it operates like the application window border, you cannot resize the document window past the border of the application window.

- **Window corner**. Operates like the application window corner, but you cannot resize the document window past the border of the application window.

Comparing Icon Types

When To Use

Read this section to learn about application icons, document icons, group items, and program item icons.

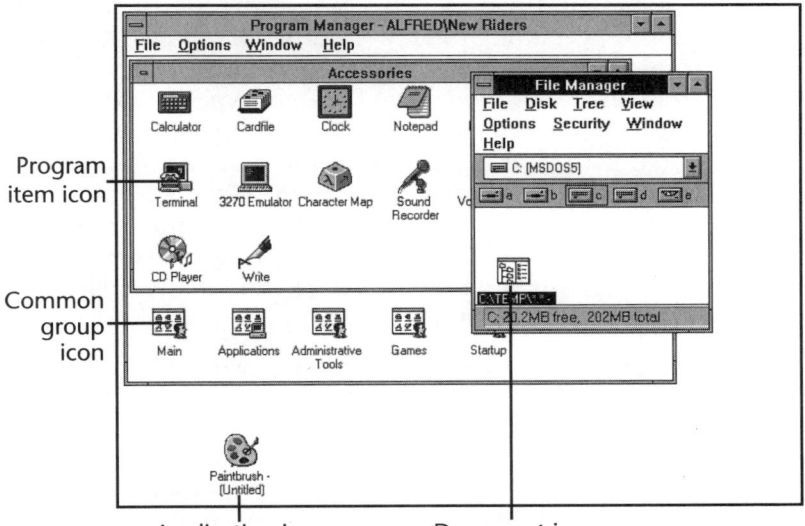

Application icon   Document icon

Notes

Icons represent applications that are available, running applications that have been minimized, or documents that have been minimized. A minimized window helps to unclutter your screen and enables an application program to run with less memory than if the window were maximized. Click on an icon to display the window's Control menu. Double-click on the icon to return the window to its previous size, shape, and position on the screen.

Windows NT contains the following icons:

- **Application icons**. Represent application windows that have been minimized. They appear along the lower edge of the desktop.

- **Document icons**. Represent document windows that have been minimized. They appear along the lower border of an application window. Document icons operate like application icons.

- **Group icons**. Represent the document windows that contain program items in Program Manager. They appear along the lower border of the Program Manager application window. In Windows NT, Program Manager uses two different types of group icons. *Personal group icons* identify groups that are stored with your log-on profile and that are displayed only when you log on to the system. You create and manage such groups. *Common group icons* identify groups that appear to everyone who works on the system and that are created and managed by the system administrator.

- **Program item icons**. Appear in the document windows within the Program Manager. They represent applications available in Windows NT. Click on a program item icon to highlight its description and move the focus to it. Double-click on a program item icon to start or load the application it represents.

Programs can use icons in other ways. File Manager, for instance, attaches an icon to each file name, directory name, and drive letter. The icons change shape and character to provide information about the status of the files, directories, and drives.

Comparing Mouse-Pointer Types
When To Use
Windows NT uses several different mouse-pointers to communicate information about your system's status. Read this section to learn about each mouse pointer and what it means.

Notes
Windows NT has eleven mouse pointers. The following sections describe them in detail.

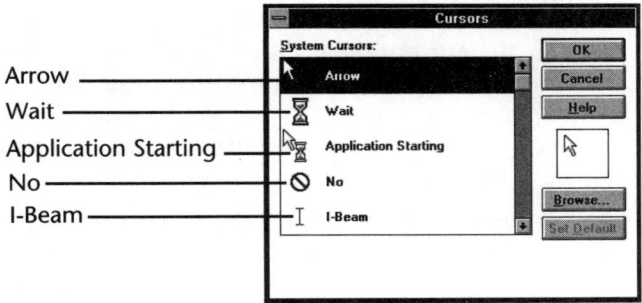

The *arrow* indicates where the mouse currently points. You can take action by clicking, double-clicking, or dragging.

The hourglass *wait* cursor indicates that the system is busy, and you must wait for the system to finish whatever it is doing before you can continue work.

In Windows NT, the hourglass appears when the mouse is over a busy application. Moving the mouse cursor outside the application often changes it to a shape that enables you to continue

working with other applications. If the
busy application is running full-screen,
press Ctrl-Esc to bring up the Task List,
and switch to another application.

The *application starting* cursor combines the arrow and
the hourglass. It indicates that an application is loading and that the system is somewhat busy while the
application loads. You can take action, however, by
clicking, double-clicking, and dragging while the
application is loading.

The *no* cursor indicates that no action is possible.
Windows NT does not display this cursor when the
system is busy and waiting for an application to finish
work. This cursor indicates that you cannot do anything at the current position of the mouse pointer. The
no cursor most commonly appears during drag-and-
drop operations to indicate that you cannot drop the
item you are dragging at the current location of the
mouse pointer.

The *I-beam* cursor appears whenever you can use the
mouse to edit a document.

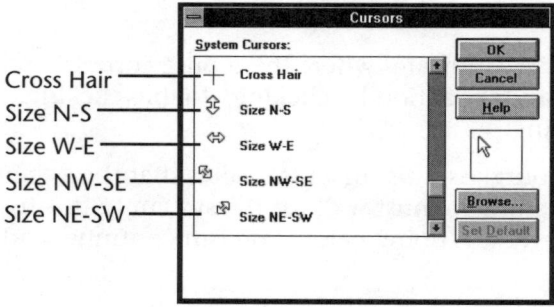

The *crosshair* cursor indicates that you can edit graphics with the cursor.

The *size* cursors appear when you can change the size of a window by dragging it with the mouse. The directions associated with a given cursor indicate the direction on the screen that you can resize the window, assuming that the top of your screen is designated as north.

Size N-S changes the vertical size of the window. Size *W-E* changes the horizontal size. Size *NW-SE* and size *NE-SW* change the vertical and horizontal dimensions at the same time. The cursor that appears depends on which corner of the window you intend to drag.

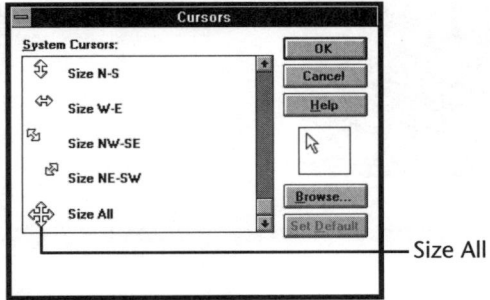

Size All

The *size all* cursor indicates that you can change all dimensions at once. It also appears when it is possible to move an object in any direction on the screen. If you select the **M**ove command on an application's Control menu, for example, the size all cursor appears.

In Windows NT, the term *mouse pointer* and *mouse cursor* are used interchangeably. In general, if you talk about mouse operations that involve pointing, clicking, and dragging, you refer to the mouse pointer. If you talk about editing actions, in which you move a cursor with the arrow keys, you refer to the mouse cursor.

Understanding the Control Menu

When To Use

Use the Control menu to perform system actions that
affect an entire window.

Steps To Follow

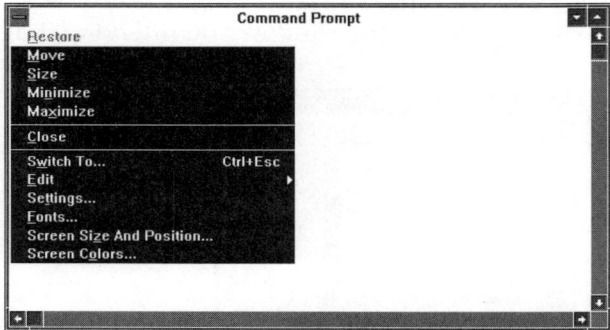

1. Open the Control menu by clicking on the Control
   menu box.

2. Take any of the following actions by clicking on its
   appropriate menu item:

   Restore. Returns the window to its previous size,
   shape, and position.

   Move. Repositions the window.

   Size. Resizes the window.

   Mi**n**imize. Shrinks the window to an icon.

   Ma**x**imize. Expands the window to full-screen size.
   (In some applications, expanding the window
   changes the action of the positioning keys.)

   Close. Closes the window.

   S**w**itch To. Activates the Task List and enables you
   to move among applications.

Edit. Appears only for DOS, OS/2, and POSIX applications. This command is described in Chapter 8.

Se**t**tings. Appears only for DOS, OS/2, and POSIX applications. This command is described in Chapter 7.

Fonts. Appears only for DOS, OS/2, and POSIX applications. This command brings up a dialog box that enables you to choose the font with which your application displays on the command-prompt screen.

Screen Si**z**e and Position. Appears only for DOS and POSIX applications. This command brings up a dialog box that enables you to choose the width and height of the command-prompt screen and its position when it is windowed.

Screen **C**olors. Appears only for DOS and POSIX applications. This command displays a dialog box that enables you to set the color attributes of the command-prompt screen.

Notes

A Control menu, which is available for every window, is attached to the Control menu box in the upper left corner of the window. Some applications display all the commands in the Control menu and dim the commands that are not currently available, others display only the commands available within the current window.

Press Alt-spacebar to open the Control menu of an application window. A good mnemonic is: the long dash in the Control box looks like the spacebar. Use Alt-hyphen to open the Control menu of a document window. A good mnemonic is: the short dash in the Control box looks like a hyphen. Use the arrow keys to move or resize a window after choosing the **M**ove or **S**ize menu items.

Arranging the Desktop

When To Use

Use the **C**ascade and **T**ile buttons in the Task List to arrange the application windows on your desktop.

Steps To Follow

1. Start the Task List application by selecting S**w**itch To from the Control menu of any application or by double-clicking on the desktop.

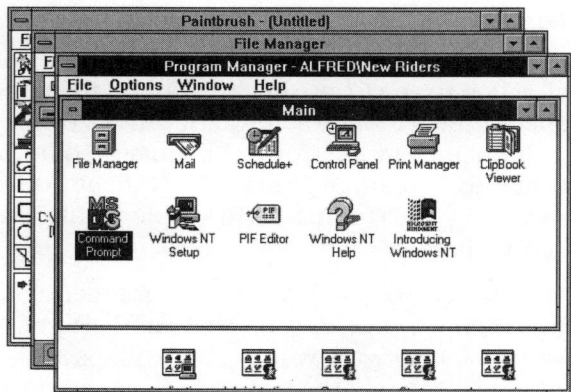

2. Click on the **C**ascade button to arrange the windows to overlap with each title bar.

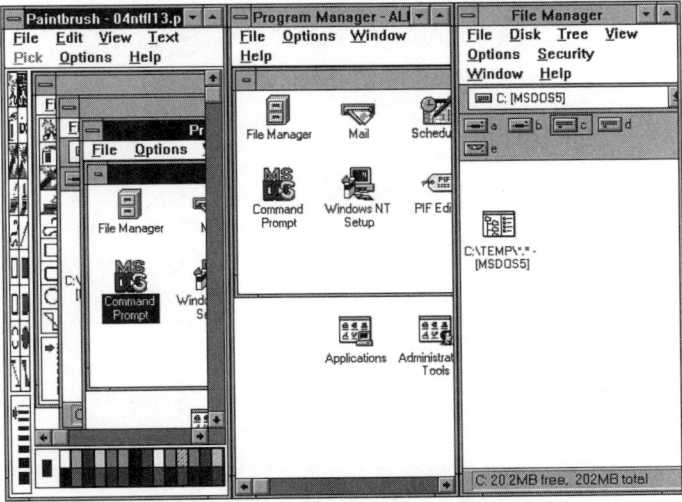

3. Click on the **T**ile button to arrange the windows on the screen like tiles on a wall.

Arranging Multiple Document Windows

When To Use

Use the **C**ascade and **T**ile commands on the application window's **W**indow menu to arrange the document windows within the application window.

Steps To Follow

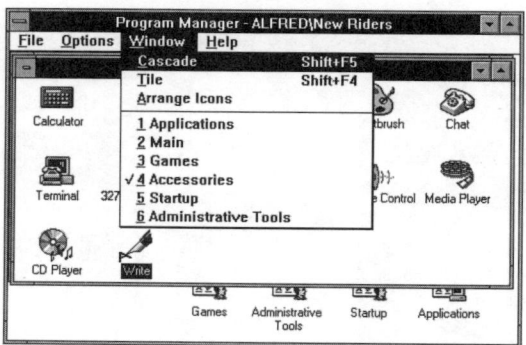

From the application window's **W**indow menu, choose
Cascade.

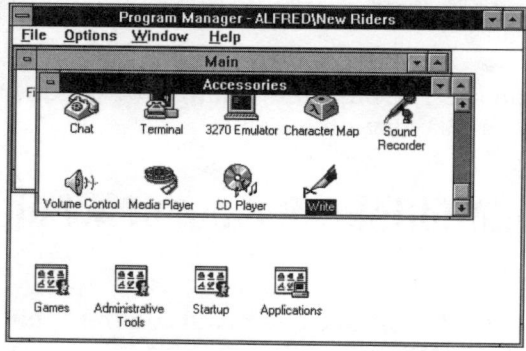

The document windows overlap, with each title bar
displayed.

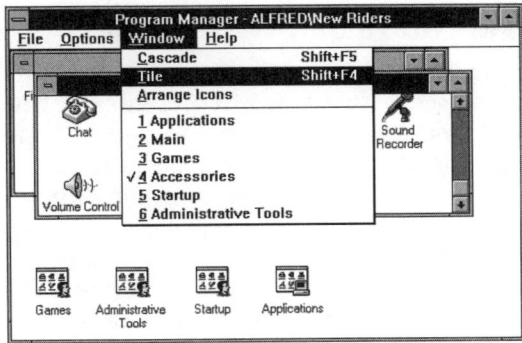

Or, from the application window's **W**indow menu, choose **T**ile.

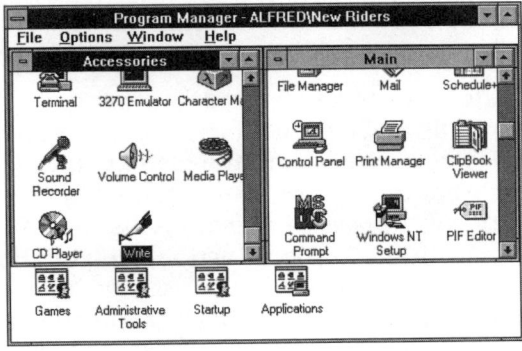

The document windows do not overlap.

Navigating within Windows NT

When To Use

Read this section to learn the most common methods of navigating within Windows NT.

Notes

The *focus* is what the currently active window or control possesses. Visually, it is represented at the application- or document-window level by a highlighted title bar. Within the workspace, the focus is represented by the flashing *insertion point*, which is the vertical line that shows where your next action will have effect. (Often this location is where all keyboard or mouse input appears.) Within a dialog box, the focused area is highlighted, or it is represented by a dotted outline box.

Navigating within Windows NT is a matter of moving and controlling the focus. The object that has the focus is the object on which you can take action. Windows NT automatically sets the focus to the workspace of an application or document window. The following list describes the most common methods:

- To activate an application window's menu, point to the menu title and click with the mouse, or press Alt. With the mouse action, the menu named by the menu title appears (or the action named by the menu title takes place if no menu is associated with the title). With the keyboard action, a highlighter appears on the menu bar. You must press the underlined letter in a menu title to make the menu appear. If you decide not to select a menu item, you must press Alt to remove focus from the menu bar.

- To move among menus on a menu bar, click on the menu title you want. You also can use the left- and right-arrow keys to move from one menu title to another or from one open menu to another. To close the current menu, click on the workspace, or press Esc. If you press Esc, the menu bar remains active, enabling you to select another menu title by pressing the underlined letter, or *hot key*. To remove the focus from the menu bar, press Alt.

- To select a menu item with a menu displayed, click on the desired menu item, or press its hot key.

Selecting a menu item executes the command associated with the menu item. This is the most common way to issue commands to an application in Windows NT. (If a menu item is followed by ellipses dots, it activates a dialog box that provides more information. If it is followed by an arrow, the menu item activates another menu, which is said to *cascade* when it appears.)

- To move among application windows and application icons, click on the application window or application icon you want to be in focus. You also can press Alt-Tab to move among application windows and application icons. Windows NT presents a dialog box that shows you the name of the application window or application icon that will come into focus after you release the Alt key. If a full-screen DOS application is in the foreground, the application is minimized so that the dialog box displaying application names can appear. The application window or icon with the focus moves to the top position on the desktop; it is often called the *current*, or *active*, application.

- To move among document windows and document icons, click on the document window or document icon you want to be in focus. You also can press Ctrl-Tab to move among document windows and document icons. The title of the document window or icon that has the focus becomes highlighted. If Program Manager has the focus, Ctrl-Tab enables you to switch among the group windows and group icons. (In some applications, notably word processors, Ctrl-Tab may have another purpose. In such cases, use the mouse or Ctrl-F6.)

- To move within the workspace, click with the mouse at the location where you want to move the insertion point. Or you can click on the scroll bars to scroll the window's workspace. You also can use the positioning keys (PgUp, PgDn, Home, End) and the arrow keys to move the insertion point.

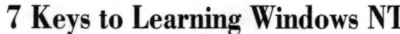

(In some applications, scrolling with a scroll bar does not move the insertion point, but scrolling with a positioning key does. This difference enables you to scroll with the scroll bars and return to your previous place by pressing a key that causes a character to be inserted in the workspace.)

- To move the focus in a dialog box, click on the dialog box control that you want, or press Tab to move the focus to the appropriate dialog box control.

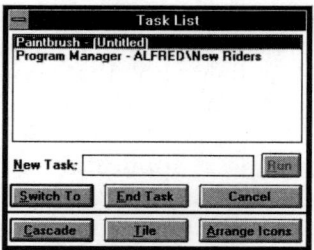

To display the Task List, double-click on the desktop, or press Ctrl-Esc. The Task List contains a list of the active applications. Double-click on an application to give it focus, or use the arrow keys to scroll through the list, and then press Enter to switch to the appropriate application.

The most efficient way to use Windows NT is to work with both the keyboard and mouse. Use the mouse to select an object you want to manipulate, and then use the keyboard to work with the object. Some applications (such as File Manager) have many mouse shortcuts. Others, such as Word for Windows, are designed for typists, and contain a wide variety of keyboard shortcuts. Use the combination of mouse and keyboard actions that you find most efficient.

Some DOS and POSIX applications have actions defined for the Windows NT movement keys. Use the application's PIF (Program Information File) to reserve a key combination for the active DOS application, rather than Windows NT.

 If an object or item appears dimmed, it is not currently available for use; it cannot be highlighted or clicked on. Applications use this technique to show which options are available at any given time. The available options often change when you select a different action. Thus, an item may be dimmed at one time and active at another.

Learning Common Keystrokes

When To Use

Use the tables in this section to learn the keystrokes assigned to various Windows NT functions.

Notes

Table 4.1 System Keys

Key or Key Combination	Function
Ctrl-Esc	Starts the Task List.
Alt-Esc	Switches to the next application window or icon.
Alt-Tab	Switches to the last application window you used, or switches

continues

Table 4.1 continued

Key or Key Combination	Function
	to the next application window. Applications running as icons are restored.
PrScr	Copies the current screen to the Clipboard.
Alt-PrScr	Copies the current application window to the Clipboard.
Alt-spacebar	Activates the Control menu for an application window.
Alt-hyphen	Activates the Control menu for a document window.
Alt-F4	Quits the current application.
Ctrl-F4	Closes the current document window.
Ctrl-F5	Restores a document window.
Ctrl-F6	Moves to the next document window.
F6	Moves to the next pane.
Shift-F6	Moves to the previous pane.
Ctrl-Shift-F6	Moves to the previous document window.
Ctrl-F7, then Arrow keys	Moves a document window.
Ctrl-F8, then Arrow keys	Sizes a document window.
Ctrl-F9	Minimizes a document window.

Key or Key Combination	Function
Ctrl-F10	Maximizes a document window.
Shift-F4	Tiles the windows on the desktop.
Shift-F5	Cascades the windows on the desktop.
Alt-Enter	Switches the execution of a DOS program from windowed to full-screen.
Arrow keys	Moves or resizes a window after you have selected **M**ove or **S**ize from the control menu.

Table 4.2 Cursor Movement Keys

Key or Key Combination	Function
Up arrow	Moves the insertion point up one line.
Down arrow	Moves the insertion point down one line.
Right arrow	Moves the insertion point right one character.
Left arrow	Moves the insertion point left one character.
Ctrl-Right arrow	Moves the insertion point right one word.
Ctrl-Left arrow	Moves the insertion point left one word.
Home	Moves the insertion point to the beginning of the line.

continues

Table 4.2 continued

Key or Key Combination	Function
End	Moves the insertion point to the end of the line.
PgUp	Moves the insertion point up one screen.
PgDn	Moves the insertion point down one screen.
Ctrl-PgUp	Scrolls the workspace left.
Ctrl-PgDn	Scrolls the workspace right.
Ctrl-Home	Moves the insertion point to the beginning of the document.
Ctrl-End	Moves the insertion point to the end of the document.

Table 4.3 Dialog Box Keys

Key or Key Combination	Function
Tab	Moves the focus from option to option within dialog boxes and menus.
Shift-Tab	Moves the focus from option to option in reverse order.
Alt-Hot key	Moves to the option or group identified by the underlined letter.
Arrow key	Moves the focus from option to option within a group of options.

Key or Key Combination	Function
Home	Moves to the first item in a list box or to the first character in a text box.
End	Moves to the last item in a list box or the last character in a text box.
PgUp	Scrolls up a list box, one screen at a time.
PgDn	Scrolls down a list box, one screen at a time.
Alt-Down arrow	Opens a list in a drop-down list box.
Spacebar	Selects an option button, or cancels a selection. Places or removes a check in a check box.
Ctrl-slash (/)	Selects all items in a list box.
Ctrl-backslash (\)	Cancels the selection in a list box, but leaves the item that currently has the focus selected.
Shift-Arrow key	Extends or cancels the selection in a text box, one character at a time.
Shift-Home	Extends or cancels the selection in a text box to the first character.
Shift-End	Extends or cancels the selection in a text box to the last character.

continues

Table 4.3 continued

Key or Key Combination	Function
Enter	Executes a command. If the focus is on an item in a list, the item is selected and then the command is executed.
Esc or Alt-F4	Cancels the dialog box without executing any commands.

Table 4.4 Editing Keys

Key or Key Combination	Function
Backspace	Deletes one character to the left of the insertion point, or deletes the selected text.
Del	Deletes one character to the right of the insertion point, or deletes the selected text.
Shift-Del	Deletes the selected text and places it on the Clipboard.
Shift-Ins	Pastes the text from the Clipboard to the place indicated by the insertion point.
Ctrl-Ins	Copies the selected text to the Clipboard.
Alt-backspace, or Ctrl-Z	Undoes the last editing keystroke.

Table 4.5 Help Keys

Key or Key Combination	Function
F1	Starts the Help windows, and displays the Help contents for the application. If the Help window is already active, it displays the Help contents for How to Use Help. In some applications, displays a Help topic for the selected command.
Shift-F1	Causes the mouse pointer to become a question mark. Press Shift-F1, and click on an object to get help for it. To get help for a keystroke, press Shift-F1 and type the keystroke. (May not be active in all applications.)

Table 4.6 Menu Keys

Key or Key Combination	Function
Alt, or F10	Activates the menu bar and selects the first item, or removes the focus from the menu.
Underlined key	Selects the command indicated by the underlined letter.
Left arrow	Moves to the next menu on the left.
Right arrow	Moves to the next menu on the right.

continues

Table 4.6 continued

Key or Key Combination	Function
Up arrow	Moves up to the next menu command.
Down arrow	Moves down to the next menu command.
Enter	Opens the selected menu, or executes the selected command.
Esc	Closes an open menu, or removes the focus from the menu.

Table 4.7 Selection Keys

Key or Key Combination	Function
Shift-Left arrow	Extends or cancels a selection one character to the left.
Shift-Right arrow	Extends or cancels a selection one character to the right.
Shift-Up arrow	Extends or cancels a selection one line up.
Shift-Down arrow	Extends or cancels a selection one line down.
Shift-PgUp	Extends or cancels a selection one screen up.
Shift-PgDn	Extends or cancels a selection one screen down.
Shift-Home	Extends or cancels a selection to the beginning of the line.
Shift-End	Extends or cancels a selection to the end of the line.

Key or Key Combination	Function
Ctrl-Shift-Left arrow	Extends or cancels a selection one word to the left.
Ctrl-Shift-Right arrow	Extends or cancels a selection one word to the right.
Ctrl-Shift-PgUp	Extends the selection left by one screen.
Ctrl-Shift-PgDn	Extends the selection right by one screen.
Ctrl-Shift-Home	Extends or cancels a selection to the beginning of the document.
Ctrl-Shift-End	Extends or cancels a selection to the end of the document.

Mastering Common Mouse Operations

When To Use

Use the table that follows to learn common mouse operations used in Windows NT.

Notes

Table 4.8 Mouse Operations

Term	Action	Response
Point	Roll the mouse until the mouse pointer is super-imposed on the item you want it to point to.	

continues

Table 4.8 continued

Term	Action	Response
Click	Press the mouse button once.	Moves the focus to the object clicked.
Double-click	Press the mouse button twice.	Moves the focus to the object clicked and executes the action associated with the object. (Example: double-click on an icon to expand it into a window.)
Drag	Hold the mouse button down, and roll the mouse.	Moves the object on the screen, or creates and extends a selection.
Drag-and-drop	Drag an object, and release the mouse button.	Moves the object on the screen, and causes an action to take place after the button is released. If the object is dropped on a second object, the action that takes place is defined by the second object. (Example: drag a file icon from File Manager, and drop it on a program item icon in Program Manager to open the related application and load the file.)

Learning Common Windows NT Controls

When To Use

Read this section to become familiar with common Windows NT *controls*, which enable you to choose options and take actions.

Notes

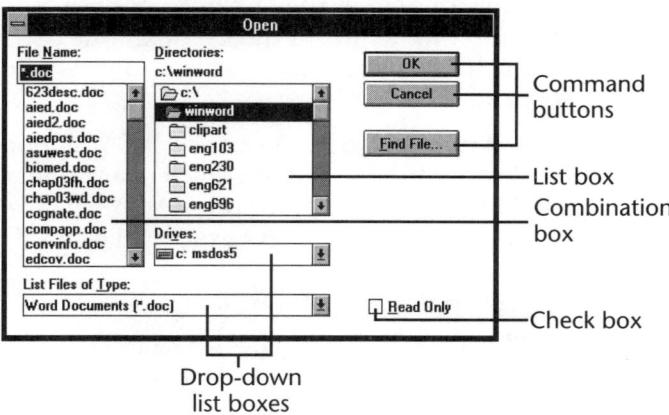

Command buttons
List box
Combination box
Check box
Drop-down list boxes

- **Command buttons**. Cause immediate execution. Click on a button, or press Alt and its underlined letter (hot key).

- **Text box**. Enables you to enter text for the current application to use. Type the text you want in the box, and press a control button to make your application take action with the text. Some text boxes have up- and down-arrow buttons at their right edges that enable you to adjust the value displayed in the text box by clicking on the arrows. Windows programmers often call these buttons *spin buttons* and the boxes associated with them *spin boxes* because you can use the buttons to spin the value showed through its possible range.

- **List box**. Presents lists of options from which you can select. Click on an option (or press Enter when it is highlighted) to select it. Use the scroll bar (or the arrow and position keys) to scroll through the list. To scroll the list to an item beginning with a specific letter, enter that letter key.

- **Combination box**. Presents a text box and a list box combined together. When you select an option in the list box, your selection is automatically added to the text box attached to the top of the list box. If the item you need does not appear on the list, you can enter it in the text box and continue your work. (Entering an item in the text box does not automatically add it to the list in the list box.) The text box and the list box function exactly as they would independently.

- **Drop-down list box**. Presents a list of options, and shows you the current choice in a rectangular box. Click on the arrow (or press Alt-down arrow) to open the list. The list works exactly like a list box.

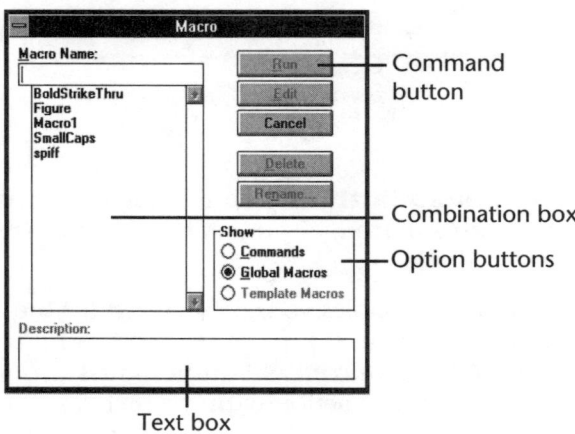

Command button

Combination box

Option buttons

Text box

- **Option buttons**. Visually present a list of mutually exclusive items. Click on an option button (or press the spacebar) to darken the button. This shows that the associated option is selected. Click (or press the spacebar) again to clear the button. This shows that the associated option is no longer selected.

- **Check box**. Presents options that you can turn on or off. Click on the check box (or press the spacebar when it is in focus) to place a check in the box. The check indicates that the option has been selected. Click on the check box (or press the spacebar when it is in focus) to remove the check. An empty check box indicates that the option has not been selected.

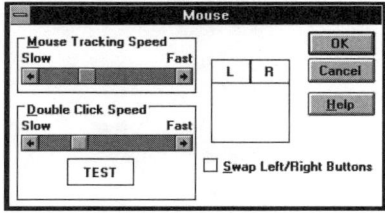

- **Scroll bars**. Often used to adjust settings, such as screen colors or mouse sensitivity, that can take a continuous range of values. Scroll bars enable you to adjust the setting and give you visual feedback about the value the setting has taken.

- **Custom controls**. Created by program designers to give their applications greater functionality than is possible with common Windows NT controls.

Customizing Windows NT

This chapter discusses the changes you can make to the way Windows NT looks and acts. You can customize Windows NT to fit your specific needs.

The information is organized into the following tasks:

- Changing the desktop colors
- Creating new desktop colors
- Changing the desktop features
- Changing the background patterns
- Changing the wallpaper
- Changing the screen saver
- Setting the cursor-blink rate
- Changing the icon spacing
- Changing the granularity
- Changing the border width
- Setting the date and time
- Controlling the system beep

- Changing the keyboard speed
- Changing the mouse speed
- Switching the mouse buttons
- Customizing the cursor
- Configuring for international use
- Changing the program icons
- Customizing the fonts
- Customizing the port settings

Changing the Desktop Colors

When To Use

Use the Color dialog box to set the color for items within the Windows NT environment. You can use an existing color scheme, or specify a color for each component.

Steps To Follow

1. From the Program Manager window, open the Main group by double-clicking on its icon.

2. Open the Control Panel by double-clicking on its icon.

3. Open the Color dialog box by double-clicking on its icon.

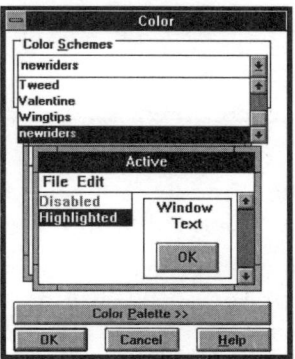

4. In the Color dialog box, select a predefined color scheme from the Color Schemes drop-down list box. The sample Windows NT items below the Color Schemes list box change color to reflect your choice.

5. Click on the OK button to accept the new color scheme. Click on the Cancel button to cancel the new color scheme selection.

6. Click on the Color Palette button to select new colors for individual Windows NT components.

7 Keys to Learning Windows NT

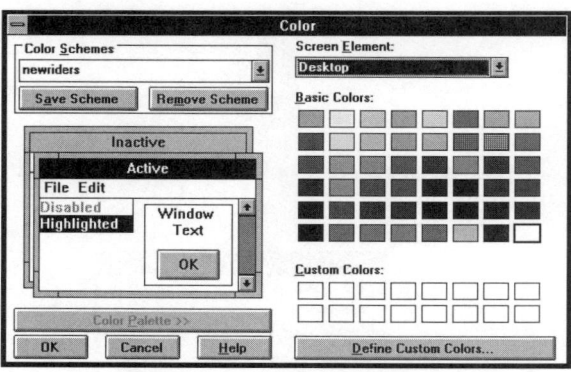

7. Select the Windows NT item you want to color from the Screen **E**lement drop-down list box.

8. Click on one of the basic colors in the **B**asic Colors control or one of the custom colors in the **C**ustom Colors control.

9. Repeat steps 7 and 8 until all of the Windows NT items are colored to your satisfaction.

10. Click on the S**a**ve Scheme button to save your new colors as a color scheme. Click on the OK button to accept the new colors.

Notes

Use colors that are easy to view in normal lighting conditions. Although a bright pink and yellow display may be striking to someone walking by your monitor, it is difficult to look at for extended periods of time.

The Color **S**chemes control lists the color schemes stored in the profile of the user who made the changes. If you create a new color scheme and save it by using S**a**ve Scheme, Windows NT adds the new color scheme to your user

profile. In this way, Windows NT can
maintain custom desktop colors for
each user who uses the system.

Creating New Desktop Colors

When To Use

Use the Custom Color Selector dialog box to create
custom colors for use in different color schemes. You
can store up to 16 colors in the Custom Colors boxes.

Steps To Follow

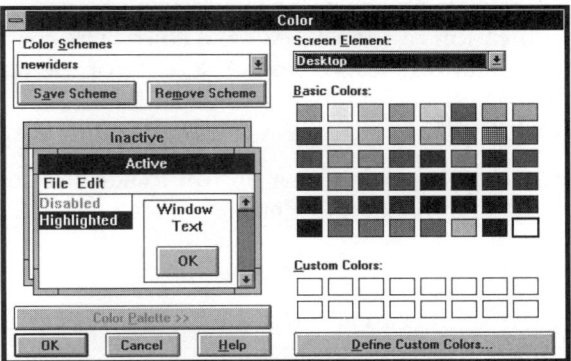

1. Click on the **D**efine Custom Colors button in the
   Color dialog box.

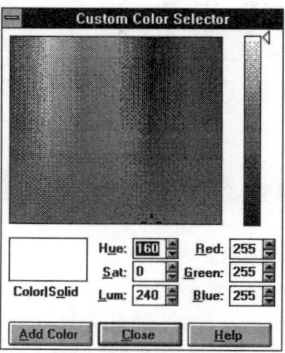

2. In the Custom Color Selector dialog box, click on the arrow buttons in the H**u**e, **S**at, **L**um, **R**ed, **G**reen, and **B**lue controls to define your new color. The arrow on the color selector chart provides an indication of the value of the color. The cursor on the color box also gives you a sense of the way the color you created relates to other colors. The Color|S**o**lid box displays the actual color you create.

3. Click on the **A**dd Color button to add the color to the **C**ustom Colors palette.

You can also use the mouse to click in the color area to select or set colors.

Notes

The information associated with the available color schemes and custom colors is stored in the user's profile. The current selections for each window component are also stored in the user's profile.

Changing the Desktop Features

When To Use

Use the Desktop dialog box on the Control Panel to change the features of the desktop layer in the Windows NT environment.

Steps To Follow

1. From the Program Manager window, open the Main group by double-clicking on the icon.

2. Double-click on the Control Panel icon.

3. Open the Desktop dialog box by double-clicking on its icon.

4. Follow the steps in the following tasks to change features of the desktop.

Notes

The features controlled by the Desktop dialog box include the pattern on the background layer, the icon spacing, the width of window borders, the grid for

sizing windows, and the rate at which the cursor blinks to indicate an insertion point.

NOTE

To change the colors of the desktop components, use the Color dialog box, as described in this chapter.

Changing the Background Patterns

When To Use

Use the Pattern control in the Desktop dialog box to select the pattern that appears on the background layer of the desktop.

Steps To Follow

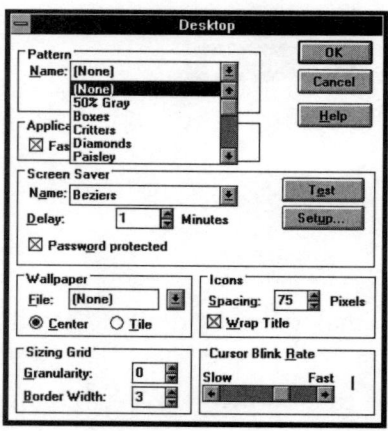

1. Use the **N**ame drop-down list box in the Desktop dialog box to select a pattern.

2. Click on the OK button to accept the new pattern.

Notes

Select a pattern from the **N**ame drop-down list box, and click on the Edit **P**attern button to edit the patterns included with Windows NT. The pattern displays in a 16×16 pixel box, in which you can modify the pattern. Your changes appear in the Sample section of the dialog box.

WARNING

You cannot edit the pattern from the keyboard—you must use a mouse to perform this step.

Changing the Wallpaper

When To Use

Use the Wallpaper control in the Desktop dialog box to select a graphic file to display on the wallpaper layer of the desktop.

Steps To Follow

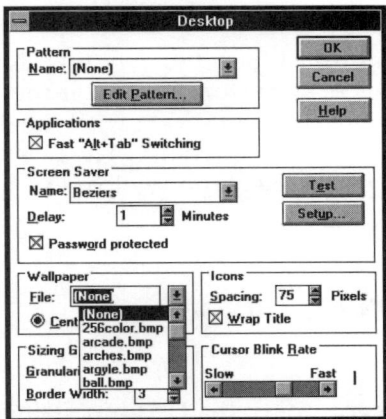

1. Use the drop-down list box in the Wallpaper control to select a new wallpaper file.

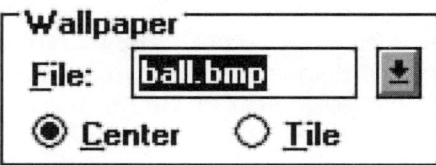

2. Click on the **C**enter option button to center the wallpaper on the screen. Click on the **T**ile option button to tile the wallpaper across the screen so that the wallpaper covers the entire screen background.

3. Click on the OK button to accept the change in the wallpaper.

Notes

Wallpaper files have a BMP extension. Use the Windows NT Paintbrush program to customize these files. If you want to create or edit wallpaper, click on the Paintbrush icon in the Program Manager's Accessories group window, select the **F**ile menu, and choose **O**pen to select one of the standard BMP files included with Windows NT.

Use Windows NT Paintbrush or other Windows NT graphics programs to create custom wallpaper files. Create the new graphics file, and save it with the BMP extension in the Windows NT directory. The new file appears the next time you select the Wallpaper drop-down list.

Changing the Screen Saver
When To Use

Use the Screen Saver control in the Desktop dialog box to select a screen saver and set its delay time.

Steps To Follow

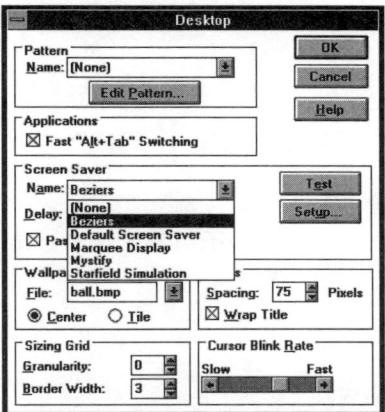

1. Use the Na̱me drop-down list box to select a
   screen saver.

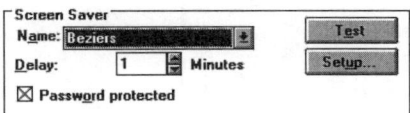

2. Enter the number of minutes before the screen saver
   should start in the Ḏelay text box. You can use the
   spin buttons at the right edge of the text box to
   adjust the displayed value.

3. Click on the Setu̱p button to change the
   customizable features of your screen saver.

4. Click on the Te̱st button to test your selected screen
   saver.

5. Check the Passw̱ord protected check box if you
   want the screen saver to lock your workstation for
   you each time it starts.

6. Click on the OK button to save your changes.

Notes

You can use Idlewild screen savers with Windows NT, as long as the IWLIB.DLL file is in your Windows NT directory (usually \WINNT).

Setting the Cursor-Blink Rate

When To Use

Use the Cursor Blink **R**ate control in the Desktop dialog box to adjust the cursor blink rate to make the cursor easier to see.

Steps To Follow

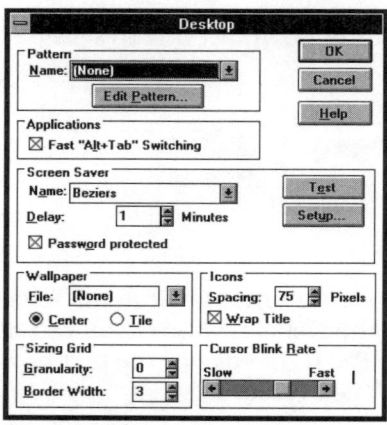

1. Drag the scroll box on the scroll bar in the Cursor Blink **R**ate control to adjust the rate. The cursor immediately to the right of the scroll bar reflects the changes you make.

2. Click on the OK button to save your changes.

Changing the Icon Spacing

When To Use

Use the Icons control in the Desktop dialog box to change the amount of spacing between icons on the screen. Increasing the space between icons makes it easier to select an icon.

Steps To Follow

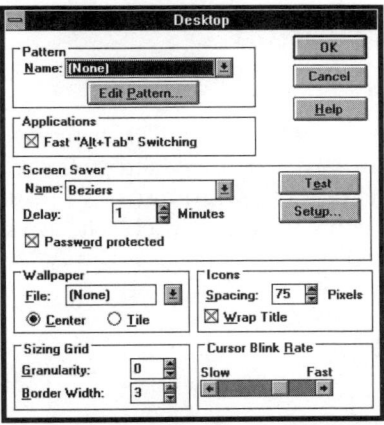

1. Adjust icon spacing by entering a new number in the **S**pacing text box. Click on the spin buttons at the right edge of the box to increase or decrease the number in the box.

2. Click on the **W**rap Title check box if you want the titles of icons to wrap to multiple lines (when the box is checked) or to keep the titles on one line (when the box is not checked).

3. Click on the OK button to save your changes.

Notes

Long titles are easier to read on your screen if you let
them wrap to the next line. If you still need more
space for the title, increase the space between icons.

TIP

Try to use the lowest spacing value
possible so that the icons occupy screen
space efficiently.

Changing the Granularity

When To Use

Use the Sizing Grid control in the Desktop dialog box
to change the granularity of the desktop. If set to a
value greater than zero, the **G**ranularity value affects
the size of the invisible grid on which windows and
icons are positioned.

Steps To Follow

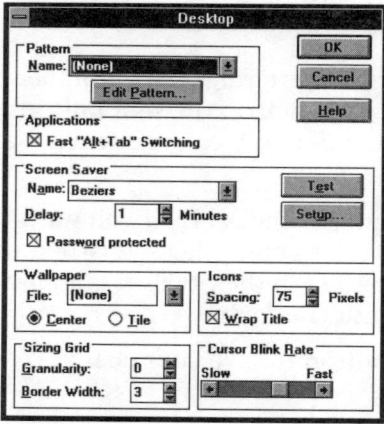

1. Adjust the granularity by entering a new number in the **G**ranularity text box. Click on the spin arrows at the right edge of the box to increase or decrease the number in the box.

2. Click on the OK button to save your changes.

Notes

Most users leave this value at the default of zero. Increase the granularity to increase the size of each cell in the grid. The windows on your screen are positioned with their upper left corner at a point on the grid. Each time you move a window with the mouse, it moves to a new point on the grid.

If you change the **G**ranularity setting, only open windows are positioned on the invisible grid.

 Modify the **G**ranularity setting if you have problems sizing windows. Start with a granularity value of 5, and experiment until you find an acceptable setting. Setting the granularity too high can make Windows NT seem jerky and can restrict your resizing options.

Changing the Border Width

When To Use

Use the Sizing Grid control in the Desktop dialog box to adjust the width of the window border. Increase the size of the border if you have difficulty positioning the mouse pointer on a window's border.

Steps To Follow

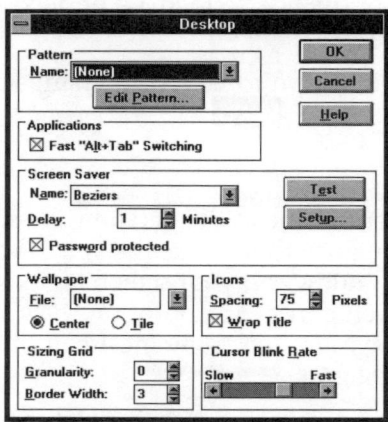

1. Adjust the border width by entering a new number in the **B**order Width text box. Click on the spin buttons at the right edge of the box to increase or decrease the number in the box.

2. Click on the OK button to save your changes.

Note

Increase the **B**order Width setting to make it easier to grab and stretch windows. On standard VGA screens, start with a setting of 5, and experiment until you find an acceptable border width.

Setting the Date and Time

When To Use

Use the Date/Time dialog box to set the system date and system clock.

Steps To Follow

1. From the Program Manager window, open the Main group by double-clicking on its icon.

2. Open the Control Panel by double-clicking on its icon.

3. Open the Date/Time dialog box by double-clicking on its icon.

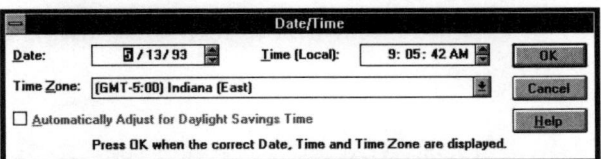

4. Click on the value that you want to change (such as the month), and type the new value or click on the spin buttons to increase or decrease the value.

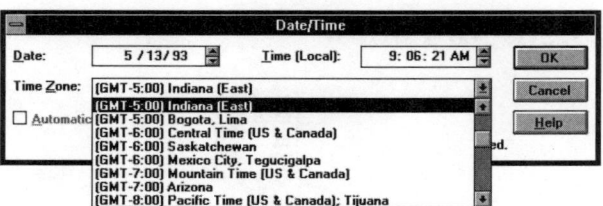

5. Use the Time **Z**one drop-down list box to select the time zone in which you reside. This setting is especially important for international communications and networking.

6. Click on the OK button to save the new date and time.

Notes

The Date/Time dialog box is functionally equivalent to the DOS DATE and TIME commands that are used from the command prompt.

Controlling the System Beep

When To Use

Use the Sound dialog box to turn the warning beep on or off.

Steps To Follow

1. From the Program Manager window, open the Main group by double-clicking on its icon.

2. Open the Control Panel by double-clicking on its icon.

3. Open the Sound dialog box by double-clicking on its icon.

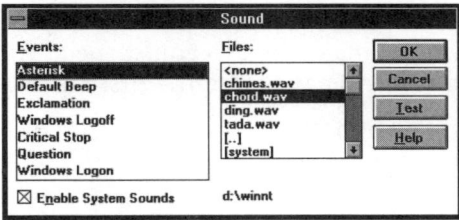

4. Click on the E**n**able System Sounds check box to turn the warning beep on (when the box is checked) or off (when the box is not checked).

5. Click on the OK button to save your changes.

Notes

The system beep sounds when certain error conditions occur. Programs that generate sound by accessing the hardware directly are not affected by this setting.

If you have a sound board installed in your computer, you can assign pre-defined or custom sounds to system events by clicking on the event in the **E**vents list box and clicking on the sound file name in the **F**iles list box. Clicking on the **T**est button enables you to hear the assigned sound. You can record and edit custom sounds with the Sound Recorder application provided with Windows NT.

Changing the Keyboard Speed
When To Use

Use the Keyboard dialog box to adjust the keyboard-repeat rate and the delay before the first repeat.

Steps To Follow

1. From the Program Manager window, open the Main group by double-clicking on its icon.

2. Open the Control Panel by double-clicking on its icon.

3. Open the Keyboard dialog box by double-clicking on its icon.

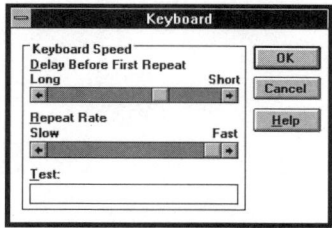

4. Drag the scroll boxes on the scroll bars to adjust the **R**epeat Rate and the **D**elay Before First Repeat. Type in the **T**est box to see how your changes affect the keyboard.

5. Click on the OK button to save your changes.

Changing the Mouse Speed

When To Use

Use the Mouse dialog box to adjust the mouse speed. Use a fast tracking speed to make the cursor move farther with each mouse movement.

Steps To Follow

1. From the Program Manager window, open the Main group by double-clicking on its icon.

2. Open the Control Panel by double-clicking on its icon.

3. Open the Mouse dialog box by double-clicking on its icon.

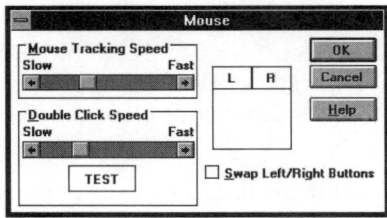

4. Drag the scroll boxes on the scroll bars to adjust the **M**ouse Tracking Speed and the **D**ouble Click Speed. Click the TEST box to see how your changes have affected the mouse.

5. Click on the OK button to save your changes.

Switching the Mouse Buttons

When To Use

Use the Mouse dialog box to swap the mouse buttons so that you can click with the right button rather than the left button. If you use the mouse with your left hand, you may find this arrangement more comfortable.

Steps To Follow

1. From the Program Manager window, open the Main group by double-clicking on its icon.

2. Open the Control Panel by double-clicking on its icon.

3. Open the Mouse dialog box by double-clicking on its icon.

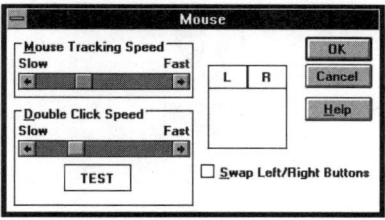

4. Check the **S**wap Left/Right Buttons check box. After the check appears, the left and right buttons have swapped functions. Verify the swap by clicking on the TEST box.

5. Click on the OK button to save your changes.

Customizing the Cursor
When To Use

Windows NT enables you to select the cursor (or mouse pointer) used by your system. Use this procedure to customize your mouse pointer.

Steps To Follow

1. From the Program Manager window, open the Main group by double-clicking on its icon.

2. Open the Control Panel by double-clicking on its icon.

3. Open the Cursors dialog box by double-clicking on its icon.

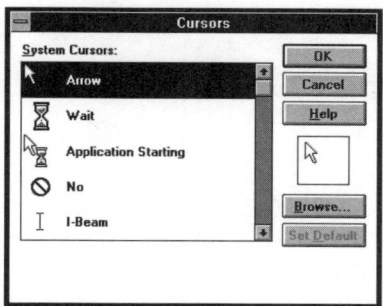

4. Select the default cursor you want to change in the **S**ystem Cursors list box.

5. Click on the **B**rowse button to view available cursors.

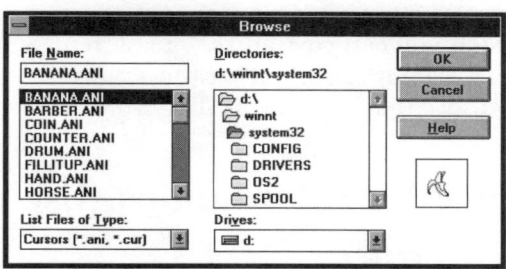

6. In the Browse dialog box, select the cursor you want by clicking on it in the File **N**ame list box. It will appear in the demonstration box on the right side of the dialog box. Click on OK to accept your choice.

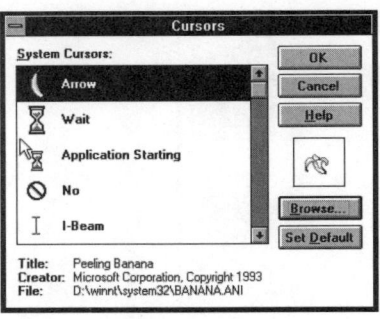

7. Click on the OK button in the Cursors dialog box to accept the changes.

Notes

Windows NT ships with a number of animated cursors with which you can customize your system. Select cursors that are meaningful for the action they represent (or those that add fun to your work).

Configuring for International Use

When To Use

Use the International dialog box to change the keyboard configuration for different languages and to specify the format for various language-dependent features.

Steps

1. From the Program Manager window, open the Main group by double-clicking on its icon.

2. Open the Control Panel by double-clicking on its icon.

3. Open the International dialog box by double-clicking on its icon.

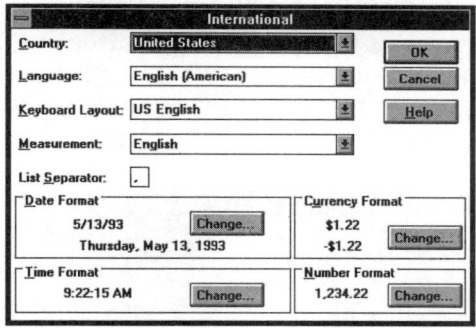

4. Use the drop-down list boxes to set the **C**ountry, **L**anguage, **K**eyboard Layout, and **M**easurement system.

NOTE

The **C**ountry you select sets other controls in this dialog box to the settings that are most common for that country. The **L**anguage setting establishes the set of letters and their sort order. The **K**eyboard Layout setting maps the keyboard into a specific arrangement that is common to a given country. (It also enables you to use the Dvorak keyboard format.) The **M**easurement setting enables you to select between English (inches and feet) and metric measurements.

5. Enter the character you want used to separate items in a list in the List **S**eparator text box.

6. Click on any of the four Change buttons to open dialog boxes that enable you to change the **D**ate Format, **T**ime Format, C**u**rrency Format, and **N**umber Format.

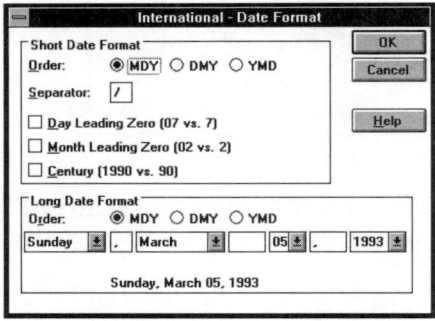

7. Use the controls in the International—Date Format dialog box to determine the order in which the date is displayed, in both long and short formats. Use the option buttons to determine the YEAR/MONTH/ DAY order. Use the check boxes and drop-down list boxes to determine the way the date is displayed. Enter the separator character you want to use in the **S**eparator text box. Click on the OK button to save your changes.

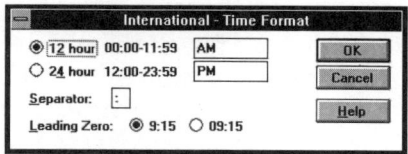

8. Use the controls in the International—Time Format
   dialog box to determine the way the time displays.
   Use the option buttons to select a 12- or 24-hour
   clock, and whether a leading zero displays. Enter the
   separator character you want to use in the **S**eparator
   text box. Click on the OK button to save your
   changes.

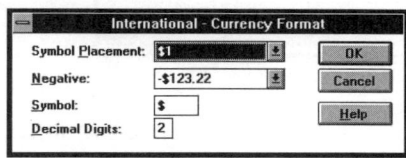

9. Use the controls in the International—Currency
   Format dialog box to determine the way currency
   amounts display. Use the drop-down list boxes to
   determine currency-symbol placement and the way
   negative numbers display. Use the text boxes to
   identify the symbol character and the number of
   decimal places that should be used. Click on the OK
   button to save your changes.

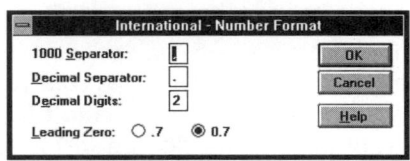

10. Use the controls in the International—Number
    Format dialog box to determine the way numbers
    display. Use the text boxes to identify the separator
    character that groups digits in numbers greater

than 999, the separator character that separates decimal fractions from the rest of the number, and the number of decimal places that are shown. Use the option buttons to determine whether a leading zero displays.

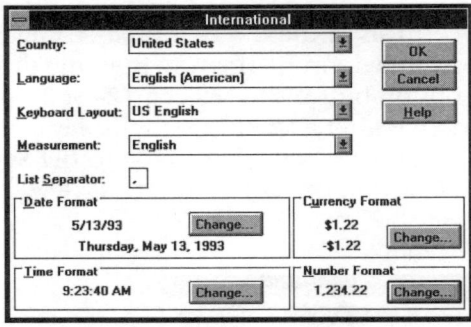

11. Click on the OK button to save your changes.

Use the Date/Time icon in the Control Panel to set the correct time and date on your system. See the section on setting the date and time in this chapter.

Changing the Program Icons

When To Use

Use the **P**roperties command on the Program Manager's **F**ile menu to change the icon that represents a program. All programs have a default icon that appears after the application (or document) is added to a Program Manager group. You can change the icon to one that you prefer or to one you have created.

 **TIP** See Chapter 6 for information on how to add an application to the Windows NT environment.

Steps To Follow

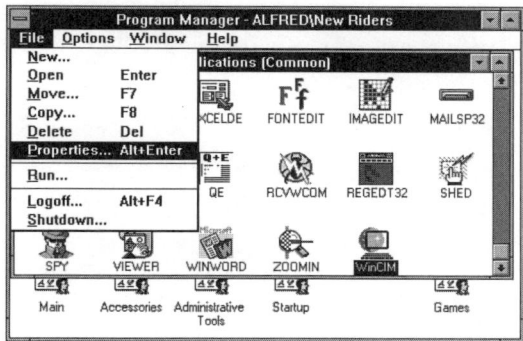

1. In Program Manager, select the program item to be changed by clicking on it once. Click on the **F**ile menu and select the **P**roperties option.

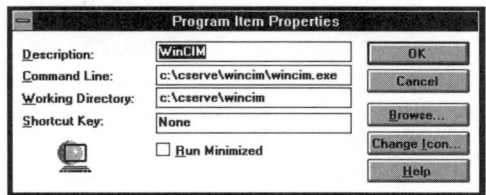

2. Click on the Change **I**con button in the Program Item Properties dialog box.

3. Drag the scroll box on the scroll bar to view any other icons that are within the current file. (If no icons are contained in the file, the dialog box displays the set of icons in the PROGMAN.EXE file.)

4. Enter a new file name in the text box to use an icon from another file, or use the **B**rowse button to search for another file using a dialog box.

5. Click on the OK button to save your changes.

Notes

The current icon and source file for the image are displayed in the Select Icon dialog box. By default, the source file is the application file associated with the icon or the PROGMAN.EXE file. (For application data files, the default file is the application associated with the icon.)

To use an icon from a different source file (an application or an icon library), you must enter the new file name and click on the OK button. A variety of sources exist for icon files, including *Maximizing Windows 3.1*, by Jim Boyce (available from New Riders Publishing). The disk included with the book contains an icon library and a program to help you create and edit icons. Icons compatible with Windows 3.1 work with Windows NT.

Customizing the Fonts

When To Use

Use the procedure described in this section to add or remove fonts from your system. You can use the fonts installed by using this procedure in Windows NT applications.

Steps To Follow

1. To add or remove display and printer fonts, open the Program Manager window, and open the Main group by double-clicking on its icon.

2. Open the Control Panel by double-clicking on its icon.

3. Open the Fonts dialog box by double-clicking on its icon.

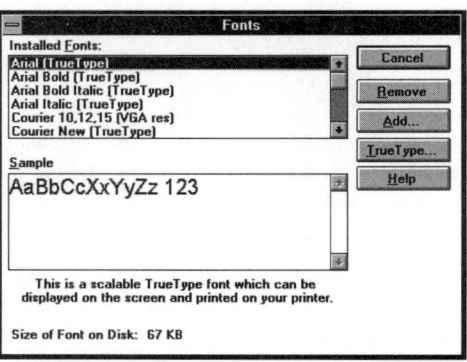

4. To remove a font, click on its name in the Installed Fonts list box. Click on the **R**emove button. Select the appropriate options in the information dialog box that appears before the font is deleted.

5. To add a font, make sure that the disk containing the fonts is inserted into your disk drive, and then click on the **A**dd button.

6. Use the drop-down list boxes to select the drive and directory on which the fonts reside. Select the fonts you want to add by clicking on them in the list box. Click on the OK button, and select the appropriate option in the information dialog box that appears.

Notes

When Setup installs Windows NT, it configures the Windows NT environment, based on the type of display driver you select. Setup installs a system font that is used as the Windows NT interface font. The information that describes this font (and all other fonts on your system) is stored in a database called the Windows NT registry, which replaces the WIN.INI and SYSTEM.INI files used by Windows 3.1.

Although you can edit font information in the Windows NT registry, most system administrators do not allow it because of the security risks involved. (If you can edit the registry, you can change the behavior of the system.) If you administer your system, editing the registry is something that Microsoft does not recommend unless absolutely necessary. You can break the operating system—quite literally. As a result, many Windows NT-compliant applications enable you to choose display fonts within their option menus.

Use the Fonts icon in the Control Panel to install or remove display and printing fonts. For each font you install, the Control Panel copies the font information to the Windows NT registry. Windows NT includes *TrueType fonts*, which provide a wide range of scalable fonts that serve for both screen display and printing. TrueType fonts provide a better *WYSIWYG* (what you see is what you get) working environment. With TrueType fonts, your file should print exactly as it appears on the screen.

Most often, fonts are stored in the \WINNT\SYSTEM32 directory. New fonts are copied to this directory, unless you uncheck the <u>C</u>opy Fonts to Windows NT Directory check box. You can deselect this box if you are low on disk space and want to use fonts that are stored on another disk drive. You can have a disk of fonts inserted in a floppy drive, for instance.

The font files shipped with Windows NT all end in an FON extension (for non-TrueType fonts) or an FOT extension (for TrueType fonts). Each TrueType font also uses a file that has a TTF extension.

Customizing Port Settings

When To Use

Use the **S**ettings button in the Ports dialog box on the Control Panel to change the settings on the serial ports.

Steps

1. From the Program Manager window, open the Main group by double-clicking on its icon.

2. Open the Control Panel by double-clicking on its icon.

3. Open the Ports dialog box by double-clicking on its icon.

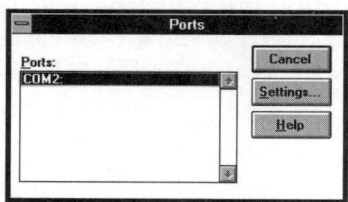

4. Click on the icon for the port you want to modify, and then click on the **S**ettings button.

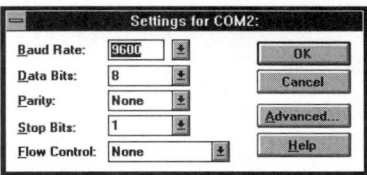

5. Use the drop-down list boxes to select **B**aud Rate, **D**ata Bits, **P**arity, **S**top Bits, and **F**low Control settings.

6. Click on the **A**dvanced button to select settings for the IRQ line or base I/O address. Use the drop-down list boxes in the Advanced Settings dialog box to select values for these settings. Click on the OK button to save your changes. (On many computers, you may not be able to make advanced settings.) If your serial communications port has the right chip set to allow advanced settings, the dialog box appears.

Notes

The settings you select for each port depend on which type of serial device (such as a modem) you have connected to it. Check the manual for your device, and set the port accordingly.

Windows NT does not allow the sharing of port addresses, interrupt requests (IRQs), or direct-memory access (DMA) channels. Therefore, Windows NT may not show all four serial ports as being available. On many machines, COM1 and COM3 share an IRQ, as do COM3 and COM4. Windows NT shows only the first port available under these circumstances.

If your mouse is installed on COM1, Windows NT does not show COM1 in the Ports dialog box.

Part Three:

Managing Applications

Program Manager

DOS, OS/2, and POSIX Applications

Program Manager

This chapter teaches you how to use the Program Manager to organize your desktop and to run application programs. You learn to create program groups and program items, to navigate among the groups and items, and to launch application programs.

The information is organized into the following tasks:

- Creating a new program group
- Creating a new program item
- Opening program groups and items
- Moving a program item
- Copying a program item
- Deleting program groups and items
- Modifying program groups and items
- Running a program
- Saving the desktop organization
- Launching programs automatically

Navigating the Program Manager

To move the focus among document windows, click on the group document window you want to bring into focus, or press Ctrl-Tab or Ctrl-F6 to move the focus among the group document windows and group icons.

You can also open or select a document window by selecting it from the **W**indow menu.

To move among program item icons, click on the desired icon, or use the arrow keys.

To open a group document window, double-click on the group icon, click on the group icon once, and press Enter; or move the focus to the group icon, and press Enter.

To close a group document window, double-click on the window's control menu box, click on the Control menu box, and then choose Mi**n**imize; click on the document window's minimize button; or press Ctrl-F4.

To launch a program, double-click on the program item icon; or click on the icon once, and choose **O**pen from the **F**ile menu. You can also move the focus to the program item icon, and press Enter.

Creating a New Program Group

When To Use

Use this procedure to create a new program group. *Program groups* are collections of applications and associated documents that are available directly from the Program Manager. These collections are contained in document windows, also called *group windows*. The Program Manager serves as the Windows NT *shell*, which is the program that provides access to the various programs in the Windows NT environment.

Steps To Follow

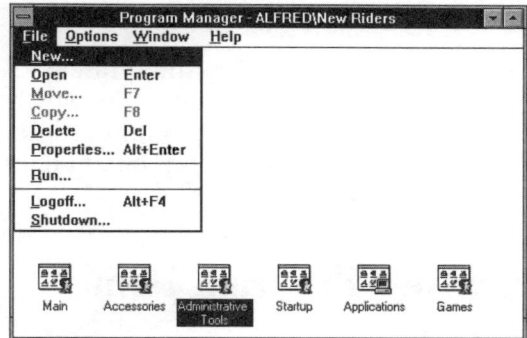

1. Click on the Program Manager's **F**ile menu, and select **N**ew.

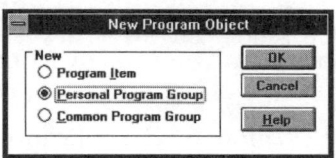

2. In the New Program Object dialog box, choose either **P**ersonal Program Group (if this group should appear only when you are logged on) or **C**ommon Program Group (if this group should appear for all users), then click on the OK button.

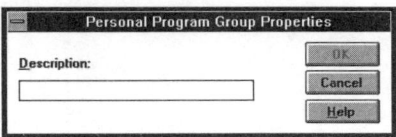

3. In the Personal Program Group Properties dialog box, enter the name you want to give the group in the **D**escription text box. This name then appears under the group icon and in the title bar of the group document window.

4. Click on the OK button.

Notes

Each program group is stored in the Windows NT registry or in an individual user's profile (which is also stored in the Windows NT registry). Information is added to the group entry for each program item that is added to the group.

Creating a New Program Item

When To Use

You must create a program item every time you add a new program or document that is accessed through the Program Manager. *Program items* are links to applications or associated documents contained within a program group. Program items are represented in group document windows by icons.

NOTE

Windows NT applications (and associated documents) display their own icons; DOS, OS/2, and UNIX applications display a generic icon. You can, however, override these icons to create your own.

Steps To Follow

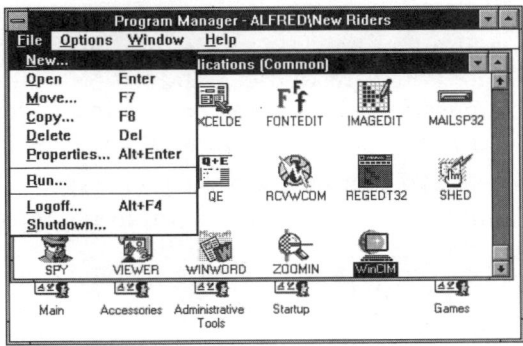

1. Click on the Program Manager's File menu, and select New.

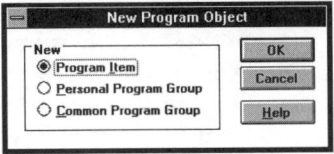

2. In the New Program Object dialog box, choose Program Item, and click on the OK button.

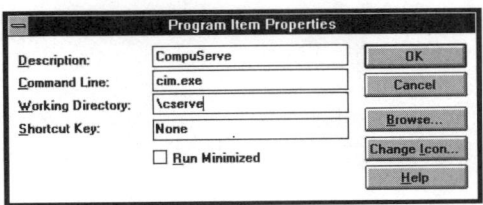

3. In the Description text box, enter the name you want to appear under the program item icon.

4. In the Command Line text box, enter the command line used to launch the application, including any switches and file names.

5. In the **W**orking Directory text box, enter the name of the working directory you want the application to use.

6. In the **S**hortcut Key text box, enter the shortcut-key sequence you want to use. Windows NT automatically translates the keys you press into the description it needs to activate a shortcut key.

7. Check the **R**un Minimized box if you always want the application to launch and run in the minimized state (as an icon).

8. Click on the OK button.

Notes

New program items are always inserted into the group document window that has the focus.

If you do not remember the exact directory path and file name for the application you want to install as a program item, use **B**rowse to search for it. **B**rowse searches a drive or directory for application files and inserts the exact path and file name in the **C**ommand Line text box.

To add an application or document to the Program Manager, use the File Manager to open the directory that contains the file. Drag-and-drop the application or document from the File Manager into the destination group or onto the group icon in the Program Manager.

For more information on the File Manager, see Chapter 9.

Make sure that the command line for DOS, OS/2, and POSIX applications references the PIF instead of the actual application-executable file.

Unless the application is in the Windows NT directory or a directory listed in your personal search path, include the entire path in the command line.

 **TIP**   For more information on setting environment variables, refer to Chapter 2.

Opening Program Groups and Items
When To Use
Use the Program Manager's **O**pen command to launch an application and open any associated document.

Steps To Follow

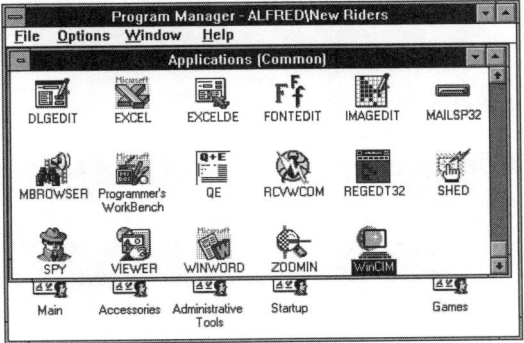

1. In the Applications (Common) dialog box, double-click on the icon you want to open.

2. If the icon is a group icon, the group document window opens.

3. If the icon is a program item icon, the application launches.

4. If the icon represents a document associated with an application, the application starts and loads the document.

Notes

You can also open an icon by using commands from the menu. Move the focus to the icon you want to open. Then, from the **F**ile menu, select the **O**pen option.

Use **O**pen to launch applications that appear as program items in the Program Manager group document window. Use **R**un to launch applications that are not installed as program items.

Moving a Program Item

When To Use

You can arrange program item icons by dragging them with the mouse.

Steps To Follow

1. Click on a program item icon and hold down the mouse button.

2. Drag the item, and drop it in the desired location. You can drop it into a new position within a group, into another group document window, or onto a group icon.

Notes

After moving a program item icon, you can rearrange the icons in a group window with the **A**rrange Icons command in the **W**indow menu. If you select **A**uto

Arrange in the **O**ptions menu, the icons arrange
themselves automatically.

To move a program item icon, click on the **F**ile menu,
and choose **M**ove. Use the drop-down list box in the
Move Program Item dialog box to choose the group to
which you want to move the icon.

Copying a Program Item

When To Use

You may want to include a program item icon in
several groups. Drag program item icons with the
mouse and the Ctrl key to copy them into additional
groups.

Steps To Follow

1. Click on the program item icon that you want to
   copy.

2. Hold down Ctrl while dragging the icon, then drop
   the icon into its new group document window or
   onto its new group icon.

Notes

You can copy your most-used programs into several
groups to ensure that the programs are readily available when you need them. You can also copy a program item by clicking on the **F**ile menu and choosing
Copy. Use the drop-down list box in the Copy Program
Item dialog box to select the group to which you want
to copy the icon.

Deleting Program Groups and Items

When To Use

Use the Program Manager's **D**elete command to remove program items or program groups.

Removing an item from the Program Manager does not delete the related application or document from your hard drive.

Steps To Follow

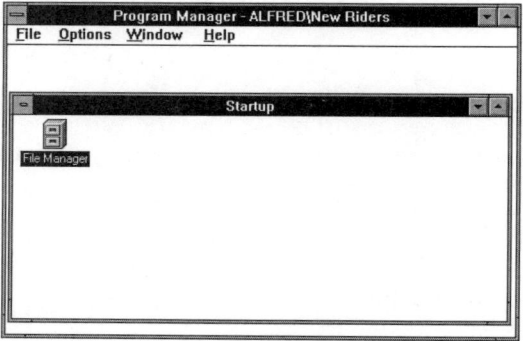

1. Click on the program item icon or group icon you want to delete.

2. Click on the Program Manager's **F**ile menu, and choose **D**elete.

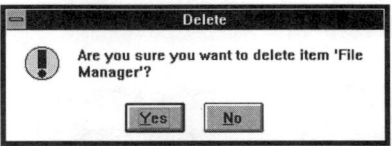

3. Click on Yes after the confirmation dialog box appears.

You can also select the icon, and then press Del.

Notes

Always delete program groups from within the Program Manager. You should never attempt to delete a program item or group by editing the Windows NT registry. In most cases, your system administrator probably has not allowed you access to the registry for security reasons.

Modifying Program Groups and Items

When To Use

Use the Program Manager's **P**roperties command to change the program item's description, command line, working directory, and shortcut key.

Steps To Follow

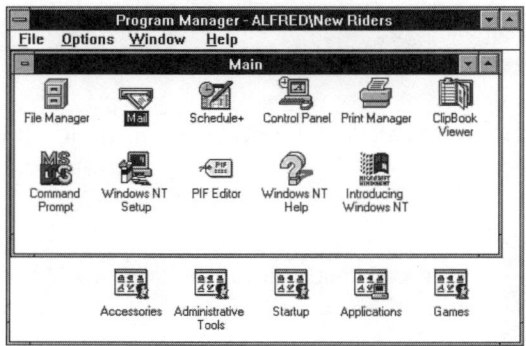

1. Click on the desired program item or group icon. If the group document window is open, click on it to make it the active window.

2. Click on the Program Manager's **F**ile menu, and choose **P**roperties (or press Alt-Enter).

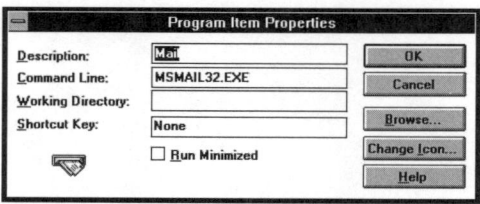

3. Modify the settings in the Program Item Properties dialog box or the Program Group Properties dialog box.

4. Click on the OK button to confirm your changes.

Notes

Information about the groups and program items in
Program Manager, as well as Program Manager's startup state, are stored in the Windows NT registry. You
should never try to modify this information by editing
the registry—make all modifications from the Program
Manager menu.

Running a Program
When To Use

Use this feature to launch a program.

Steps To Follow

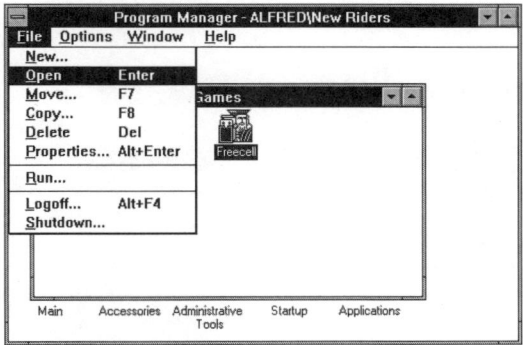

1. If the program is included in a group document
   window, double-click on the window to open it. To
   launch the program, double-click on the program
   item icon, or click on the icon once and choose
   Open from the Program Manager's **F**ile menu.

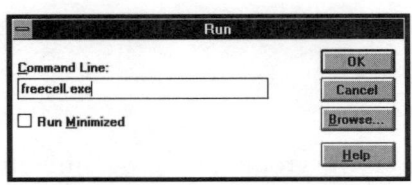

2. If the program is not included in a group document
    window, select the **R**un option from the Program
    Manager's **F**ile menu. In the Run dialog box, enter
    the name of the application's executable file in the
    text box. Include the directory path if the program
    is not in a directory on your personal search path.

Saving the Desktop Organization

When To Use

If you have arranged the background, colors, and
program groups on your desktop, you may want to
save this setup when you exit.

Steps To Follow

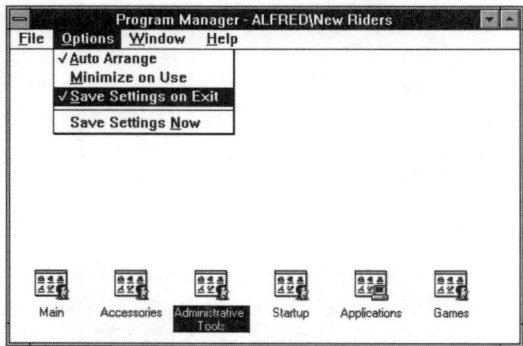

From the Program Manager's **O**ptions menu, choose
Save Settings on Exit.

Notes

If you want to save settings immediately without exiting, choose the Save Settings **N**ow option on the **O**ptions menu.

Launching Programs Automatically

When To Use

Use this feature to launch programs automatically when Windows NT starts up.

Steps To Follow

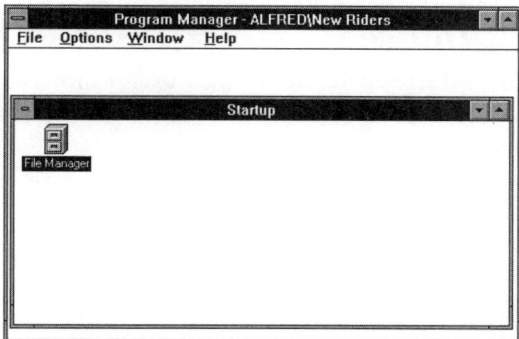

1. Copy or move the program item icons for the programs you want to launch automatically to the Startup program group.

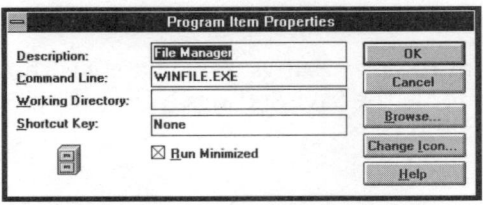

2. If you want the program to run as an icon when it launches, check the **R**un Minimized box in the Program Item **P**roperties dialog box.

Notes

Even though you can find files called WIN.INI and SYSTEM.INI on your hard drive in the Windows NT directory, you should not use these files to control the behavior of Windows NT. They are provided only for compatibility with 16-bit Windows applications. As a result, the `run=` and `load=` lines in WIN.INI that you may have used in the past are no longer available. Use the Startup group to launch programs automatically.

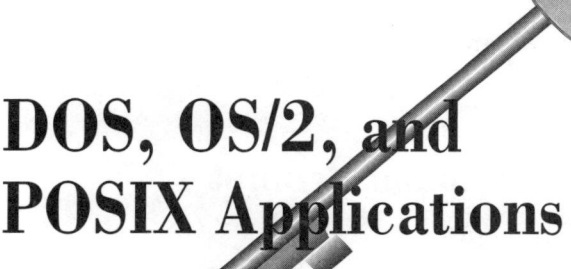

DOS, OS/2, and POSIX Applications

This chapter discusses running DOS, OS/2, and POSIX applications under Windows NT. Each type of application is handled somewhat differently. Windows NT sets up a compatible environment for each type of program and allocates the appropriate type of memory for it.

DOS applications require a Program Information File (PIF) to run under Windows NT. You learn to create a PIF that describes the application to Windows NT and to adjust Windows NT so that it can run your DOS, OS/2, or POSIX application most effectively. OS/2 and POSIX applications do not require a PIF. You learn how to run these applications from the Program Manager and from the command prompt.

The information is organized into the following tasks:

- Using the command prompt
- Creating a PIF to run a DOS application
- Creating a PIF for Standard mode
- Creating a PIF for 386-Enhanced mode
- Modifying a PIF
- Running programs
- Terminating a DOS, OS/2, or POSIX application

Using the Command Prompt
When To Use
Use the Command Prompt icon to issue a command or series of commands in the Windows NT environment.

Steps To Follow

1. From the Program Manager window, open the Main program group by double-clicking on its icon.

2. Start a new command session by double-clicking on the Command Prompt program item icon.

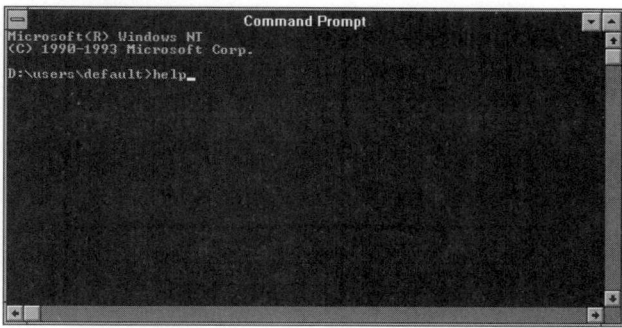

3. In the Command Prompt dialog box, enter commands at the command prompt.

4. After you finish working at the command prompt, type **Exit** at the prompt to return to Windows NT.

Notes

You can also exit a command session by double-clicking on the command window's control menu box.

Windows NT offers a set of commands that are based on DOS commands. To find out which commands can be used, type **Help** at the command prompt, and press Enter.

If a command-prompt session crashes, and you cannot issue commands from the keyboard, press Alt-Enter to place the command-prompt session in a window, and double-click on the control menu box. This action closes the command-prompt session and returns you to Windows NT.

Creating a PIF To Run a DOS Application

When To Use

Use this task to create a custom Program Information File (PIF) for a DOS application. A PIF file tells Windows NT how to run a non-Windows application.

Steps To Follow

1. From the Program Manager window, open the Main group by double-clicking on its icon.

2. Double-click on the PIF Editor program item icon.

3. Follow the directions for creating a PIF for Standard mode or for 386-Enhanced mode in this chapter, depending on which Windows operating mode you use.

Standard mode is not actually used by Windows NT, but Windows NT enables you to specify these options in case you want to create a PIF to work with an application running under Windows 3.1 Standard mode.

Notes

Every DOS application requires an associated PIF file to run under Windows NT. Windows NT includes a default PIF file that works with most DOS programs. Creating a custom PIF file gives you control over the way Windows NT constructs the DOS environment in which your DOS application runs.

Use the PIF Editor to create the PIF (unless one was included with the application) and the Program Manager's **N**ew command to associate it with a program item icon. If no PIF is explicitly assigned to a program, the default PIF (_DEFAULT.PIF) is used.

Custom PIF files are most often used to enhance performance or to set a default environment specification.

Each PIF contains separate settings for multitasking (within 386-Enhanced mode) and for task-swapping (within Standard mode). A new PIF is assigned the values that are contained in the default PIF for both environments. If you modify only one of the two sets of information (*multitasking*), the other set retains the default settings (*task-swapping*).

Creating a PIF for Standard Mode

When To Use

Read this section to learn to set PIF settings for a DOS program in Standard mode that will run under Windows 3.1.

NOTE   Windows NT provides access to Standard mode settings only for creating PIFs that can be used with Windows 3.1.

Steps To Follow

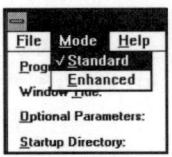

1. In the PIF Editor dialog box, click on the **M**ode menu, and select the **S**tandard option.

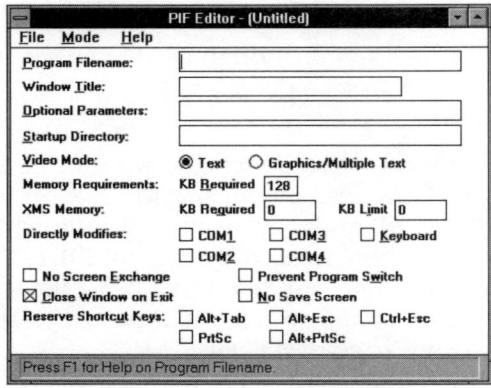

2. Use the controls shown in the figure to enter the settings for your application. The controls are explained in the Notes that follow.

Notes

Use the **P**rogram Filename text box to enter the name of the program's executable file. You should include the full path to the program if the program does not reside in a directory specified in your DOS PATH setting. You can enter an environment variable here and set its value in your AUTOEXEC.BAT file. Enclose environment variables in percent signs (for example, %WORD%).

Use the Window **T**itle text box to enter the information you want displayed in the title bar when the application runs in a window. In Standard mode, you see the title-bar information if you press Alt-Tab to switch among applications. If you enter nothing here, the title bar displays the name of the PIF without the extension. As with **P**rogram Filename, you can enter an environment variable in this text box and set its value in AUTOEXEC.BAT.

Use the **O**ptional Parameters text box to enter information you want passed to the application as if it were part of the command line. Use this text box for command-line switches. (You enter a file name here only if you always want to load that file whenever you launch the application.) Enter a question mark (**?**) if you want Windows 3.1 to prompt you for optional parameters. As with **P**rogram Filename, you can enter an environment variable in this text box and set its value in AUTOEXEC.BAT.

Use the **S**tartup Directory text box to enter the directory that will be made current before the application launches. As with **P**rogram Filename, you can enter an environment variable in this text box and set its value in AUTOEXEC.BAT.

Some applications switch to a new directory as part of their startup process, which overrides this setting.

Use the **V**ideo Mode option buttons to select Graphics/ Multiple Text or Text mode. In *graphics mode*, more memory is reserved for the application. Use graphics mode only when the application will not run in text mode.

NOTE

Multiple text mode is for applications that display text on more than one video page. *Text mode* is used by applications that display only ASCII text on the screen in an 80×24 grid of character cells.

Use the Memory Requirements: KB **R**equired text box to enter the amount of conventional memory that must be available for the application to launch.

Use the XMS Memory: KB Re**q**uired text box to enter the minimum amount of extended memory necessary to launch an application. You ordinarily do not change this setting unless an application must control a specified amount of extended memory to run. Entering a number other than zero (0) increases the amount of time necessary for task-swapping.

The XMS Memory: KB L**i**mit text box contains the maximum amount of extended memory that the application can control. A value of -1 permits the application to control all available extended memory. Enter a number in this box if you want to limit the amount of extended memory an application can control. A zero (0) setting means that the application cannot control any extended memory.

Use the Directly Modifies check boxes to indicate each port that the application needs to control. Check the **K**eyboard box to indicate that only the application, not Windows 3.1, has exclusive control of the keyboard. You cannot task-swap, and you must exit the application to return control of the keyboard to Windows 3.1.

Use the No Screen **E**xchange check box to disable Windows 3.1's capability to capture a screen image with the Print Screen (PrtScr) key. Disable this feature to conserve memory allocated for screen-capture buffers.

The Prevent Program S**w**itch check box disables task-swapping from the application. When it is checked, you must exit the application to return to Windows 3.1. Disable this feature to conserve memory allocated for task-swapping buffers.

If you do not want information to be saved on the screen during task-swapping, check the **N**o Save Screen box. Normally, Windows 3.1 saves this information so that it can be displayed correctly when you return to the application. Disabling this feature conserves the memory allocated to saving the screen.

 If you disable the Screen Save feature, the screen may not display correctly when you return to the application.

The **C**lose Window on Exit check box should be unchecked if information is to be displayed after you exit the application. If you assign DOS commands to an icon with a PIF, you must remove the check in this box to see the command's output.

The Reserve Shortc**u**t Keys boxes, when checked, enable an application to use keystrokes that are normally reserved for Windows NT to use exclusively.

Remember, Standard-mode PIFs are for use with Windows 3.1 only. PIFs for use with Windows NT should be Enhanced-mode PIFs. Standard-mode options were retained in the PIF Editor only so that compatible PIFs can be created without exiting Windows NT and starting Windows 3.1.

Creating a PIF for 386-Enhanced Mode

When To Use

Read this section to learn to set PIF settings for a DOS program in 386-Enhanced mode.

Steps To Follow

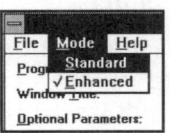

1. Click on the PIF Editor's **M**ode menu, and select the **E**nhanced option.

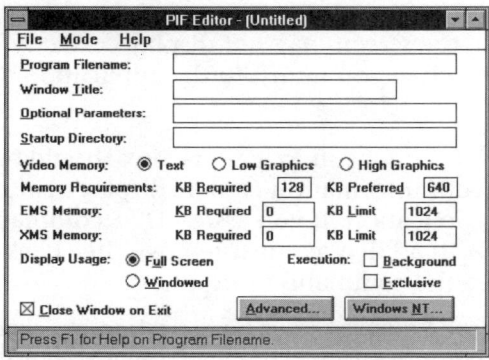

2. Use the controls shown to enter the settings for your application. The controls are explained in the Notes that follow.

3. Use the **A**dvanced and Windows **N**T buttons to enter the advanced settings and Windows NT settings for your application. They are also explained in the Notes that follow.

Notes

Basic Options

In the **P**rogram Filename text box, enter the name of the application associated with the PIF. The name must have a BAT, COM, or EXE extension. You can enter an environment variable in this text box and set its value in the AUTOEXEC.BAT file. Enclose environment variables in percent signs (for example, %WORD%).

In the Window **T**itle text box, enter the information you want displayed in the title bar when the application runs in a window. If you enter nothing here, the title bar displays the name of the PIF without the extension. You can enter an environment variable in this text box and set its value in AUTOEXEC.BAT. Enclose environment variables in percent signs (for example, %WORDTITLE%).

Use the **O**ptional Parameters text box to enter information you want passed to the application as if it were part of the command line. Use this text box for command-line switches. (You enter a file name here only if you always want to load that file when you launch the application.) Enter a question mark (**?**) if you want Windows NT to prompt you for optional parameters. You can enter an environment variable in this text box, and set its value in AUTOEXEC.BAT. Enclose environment variables in percent signs (for example, %WORDPAR%).

Use the **S**tartup Directory text box to enter the directory that will be made current before the application launches. As with **P**rogram Filename, you can enter an environment variable in this text box, and set its value in AUTOEXEC.BAT.

Some applications switch to a new directory as part of their startup process, which overrides this setting.

Use the **V**ideo Memory option buttons to determine the way your application is displayed initially and how much memory is allocated for the video display. The Text option enables the application to display in text mode, and requires the least memory. Low Graphics enables the application to display in CGA graphics mode, and requires approximately 32K of memory. High graphics enables the application to display in high-resolution VGA mode, and requires approximately 128K of memory. (Windows NT does not use this setting. It is provided only for compatibility with Windows 3.1.)

Use the Memory Requirements: KB **R**equired text box to enter the amount of conventional memory that must be available before the application can be launched. A value of -1 gives the application all available conventional memory. You can use this setting to make sure that enough conventional memory is available to launch other applications. In general, it is best to leave it set to 128.

Use the Memory Requirements: KB Preferre**d** text box to enter the maximum amount of conventional memory that can be allocated to an application. Windows NT gives the application no more than this amount. A value of -1 gives the application all available conventional memory.

Use the EMS Memory: **K**B Required text box to enter the minimum amount of expanded memory necessary to launch an application. The default value of zero (0) is usually the best option, unless your application must have a specified amount of expanded memory to run.

Use the EMS Memory: KB **L**imit text box to enter the maximum amount of expanded memory that Windows NT can give your application. A value of -1 provides an application with as much expanded memory as it requests, up to the limit of system memory.

Use the XMS Memory: KB Re**q**uired text box to enter the minimum amount of extended memory necessary to launch an application. The default value of zero (0) is usually the best option, unless your application must have a specified amount of extended memory to run.

Use the XMS Memory: KB Limit text box to enter the maximum amount of extended memory that Windows NT can give your application. A value of -1 provides an application with as much extended memory as it requests, up to the limit of system memory.

The Display Usage option buttons control the way your application initially appears, Full Screen or Windowed (in a window). To go back and forth between these two display options, press Alt-Enter.

Graphical applications can run full-screen only on x86-based computers. On RISC-based computers, DOS applications can run only in a window.

The Execution check boxes determine whether your application can run in the background and whether it enables other applications to run in the background. Check the Background box to set your application to run, even when it is not the active application. Check the Exclusive box to suspend all other applications when your application is active, even if the other applications have their Background box checked. (Windows NT does not use these settings. They are provided for compatibility with Windows 3.1 only.)

The Close Window on Exit check box should be unchecked if you want an application's window to remain on-screen after the application terminates. Deselect this option if the application leaves information on-screen after it terminates. If you assign DOS commands to an icon with a PIF, you must remove the check in this box to see the command's output. (Windows NT does not use this option. It is provided for compatibility with Windows 3.1 only.) Type **Exit** to close the window.

Advanced Options

```
┌─────────────────────────────────────────────────────────┐
│                    Advanced Options                       │
│ ┌─Multitasking Options──────────────────────┐  ┌──────┐  │
│ │ Background Priority: [50]  Foreground Priority: [100] │  OK  │  │
│ │           ☒ Detect Idle Time              │  ┌──────┐  │
│ │                                            │  Cancel  │  │
│ ┌─Memory Options────────────────────────────────────────┐│
│ │ □ EMS Memory Locked      □ XMS Memory Locked          ││
│ │ ☒ Uses High Memory Area  □ Lock Application Memory    ││
│ ┌─Display Options───────────────────────────────────────┐│
│ │ Monitor Ports: □ Text  □ Low Graphics  □ High Graphics││
│ │        ☒ Emulate Text Mode  □ Retain Video Memory     ││
│ ┌─Other Options─────────────────────────────────────────┐│
│ │ ☒ Allow Fast Paste        □ Allow Close When Active   ││
│ │ Reserve Shortcut Keys: □ Alt+Tab □ Alt+Esc □ Ctrl+Esc ││
│ │                        □ PrtSc  □ Alt+PrtSc □ Alt+Space││
│ │                        □ Alt+Enter                    ││
│ │ Application Shortcut Key:  [None]                      ││
│ ┌──────────────────────────────────────────────────────────┐
│ Press F1 for Hel│ Custom MS-DOS Initialization Files ─────     │  ┌──────┐ │
│                 │ Autoexec Filename: [D:\WINNT\SYSTEM32\AUTOEXEC.NT]  OK    │
│                 │ Config Filename:   [D:\WINNT\SYSTEM32\CONFIG.NT]  ┌──────┐ │
│                 │                                             │  Cancel  │ │
│                 │ Press F1 for Help on Autoexec Filename.      │
└──────────────────────────────────────────────────────────────┘
```

The options in the following list determine the way
applications run in relationship to one another:

- **B**ackground Priority contains a number that represents the amount of processor time that an application receives when it is not active. (Windows NT
  does not use this setting. It is provided for compatibility with Windows 3.1 only.)

- **F**oreground Priority contains a number that represents the amount of processor time an application
  receives when it is active. (Windows NT does not
  use this setting. It is provided for compatibility with
  Windows 3.1 only.)

- **D**etect Idle Time enables Windows to give resources
  to other applications when this application is idle.
  (Windows NT does not use this setting. It is provided for compatibility with Windows 3.1 only.)

The following check boxes control the way your
application controls memory resources:

- EMS Memory Lo**ck**ed prevents your application's expanded memory from being swapped to disk. (Windows NT does not use this setting. It is provided for compatibility with Windows 3.1 only.)

- XMS Memory L**o**cked prevents your application's extended memory from being swapped to disk. (Windows NT does not use this setting. It is provided for compatibility with Windows 3.1 only.)

- **L**ock Application Memory prevents your application's conventional memory from being swapped to disk. (Windows NT does not use this setting. It is provided for compatibility with Windows 3.1 only.)

- Uses **H**igh Memory Area enables an application to make use of the *high-memory area*, which is the first 64K above conventional memory. This option can save time, but it ties up system resources. (Windows NT does not use this setting. It is provided for compatibility with Windows 3.1 only.)

The following check boxes determine the way your application uses video memory:

- Monitor Por**t**s informs Windows that it must check the video I/O ports when it switches to or from your application while running in any of the three screen modes. Check these boxes only if your application does not display correctly when you switch away from it and return to it. (Windows NT does not use this setting. It is provided for compatibility with Windows 3.1 only.)

- **E**mulate Text Mode speeds up the display of text. (Windows NT does not use this setting. It is provided for compatibility with Windows 3.1 only.)

- Retain Video **M**emory prevents Windows from freeing unused video memory for use by other applications. Check this box if your application can change video mode while it is running. (Windows NT does not use this setting. It is provided for compatibility with Windows 3.1 only.)

In general, leave these boxes at their default settings (all unchecked except **E**mulate Text Mode) unless you experience problems with your application.

The following controls alter various aspects of Windows NT's interaction with your application:

- Allow Fast **P**aste enables your application to receive information pasted from the Clipboard at the fastest rate. (Windows NT does not use this setting. It is provided for compatibility with Windows 3.1 only.)

Unselect Allow Fast **P**aste only if you experience problems pasting information into your application.

- Allow **C**lose When Active enables you to exit Windows NT without closing your DOS application with its Exit command. (Windows NT does not use this setting. It is provided for compatibility with Windows 3.1 only.)

Do not check Allow **C**lose When Active unless you are absolutely sure that your application uses standard DOS file handles. If it does not use standard DOS file handles, you can lose data if you check this box.

- Reserve **S**hortcut Keys enables an application to use keystrokes that are normally reserved for Windows NT to use exclusively.

- **A**pplication Shortcut Key assigns the shortcut key you want to use to access your application. Bring

this text box into focus, and enter the keystrokes
you want to use. Windows NT translates them into
the descriptions it needs to create the shortcut key,
and displays these descriptors in the text box.

Windows NT Options

The Windows NT Options dialog box enables you to
enter the name of an AUTOEXEC.BAT file and a
CONFIG.SYS file for use with the application. By
default, Windows NT uses its own configuration files,
AUTOEXEC.NT and CONFIG.NT, as the bases for
creating configuration files for use with a DOS application. You can specify other configuration files to use in
the text boxes in this dialog box. In this way, each of
your DOS applications can set up a custom environment for itself.

Modifying a PIF
When To Use
Use the PIF Editor to modify existing PIF files to tailor
a DOS application for your system configuration.

Steps To Follow

1. From the Program Manager window, open the Main
   program group by double-clicking on its icon.

2. From the Main group document window, double-click on the PIF Editor program item icon.

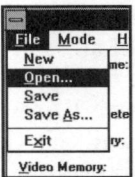

3. Click on the PIF Editor's **F**ile menu, and select the **O**pen option.

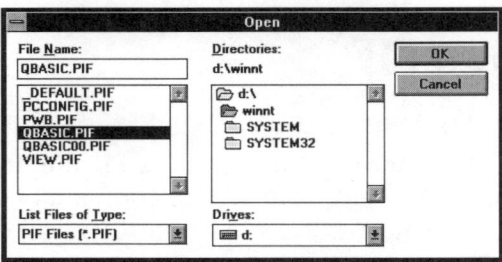

4. In the Open dialog box, click on the PIF that you want to modify, and then click on the OK button.

5. In the PIF Editor, modify the settings in the various controls.

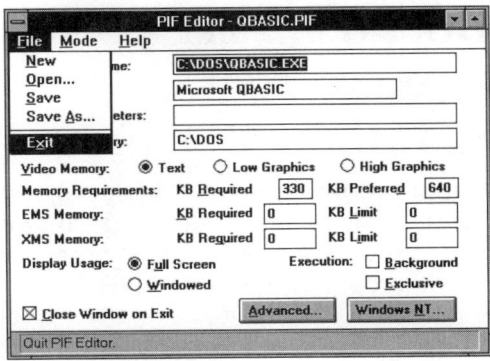

6. After you finish editing, click on the **F**ile menu, and select the E**x**it option.

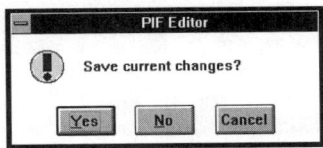

7. In the confirmation dialog box, click on the **Y**es button to save your changes.

Notes

If the DOS application's directory is listed in the DOS PATH environment variable, you do not need to specify the program's full path name in the **P**rogram Filename text box.

Running DOS, OS/2, and POSIX Programs

When To Use

To launch applications, double-click on program item icons or use the Program Manager's **R**un command. In the **R**un command's dialog box, specify the program's name (for DOS programs, specify its PIF).

Steps To Follow

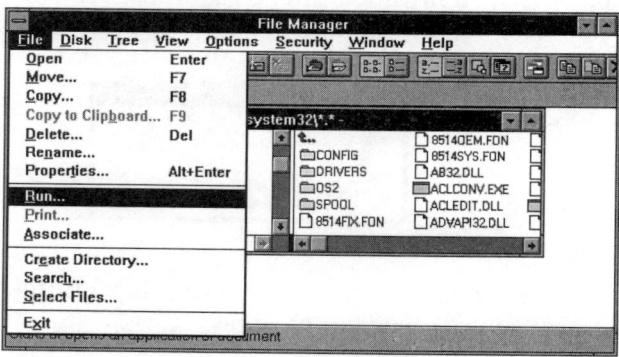

1. In the File Manager or the Print Manager, click on the **F**ile menu, and select the **R**un option.

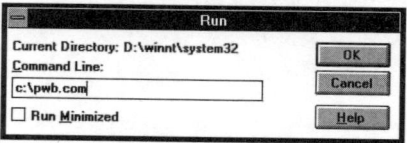

2. In the Run dialog box, enter the name of the application to be executed, including the directory path if the application is not in a directory on the search

path. If the Run **M**inimized check box is checked, the application launches as an icon.

Notes

You can use the **B**rowse button to search for executable files if you cannot remember the exact file name or directory location of the application you want.

 Remember to specify the PIF for a DOS application.

You can also run a DOS, OS/2, or POSIX application by starting the command prompt, typing the program's executable file name at the command prompt, and pressing Enter.

 If you are in the File Manager, you can launch any application by double-clicking on its executable file or on any document file associated with the application. Click on a document file to automatically load it.

Terminating a DOS, OS/2, or POSIX Application

When To Use

Use the instructions in this section only when a DOS, OS/2, or POSIX application has locked up.

Steps To Follow

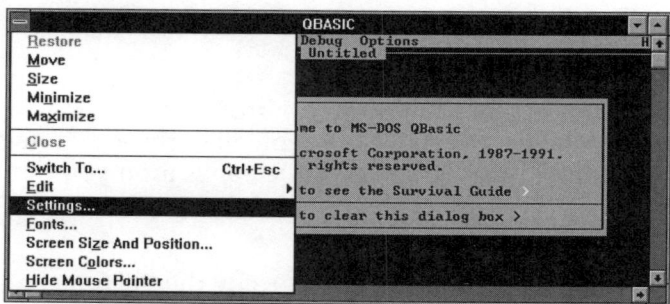

1. Click on the Control menu box of the application you want to terminate, and select the Se**t**tings option from the Control menu.

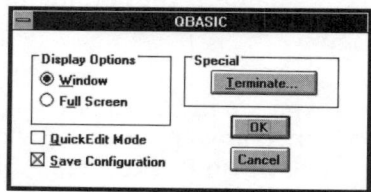

2. Click on the **T**erminate button in the dialog box that appears.

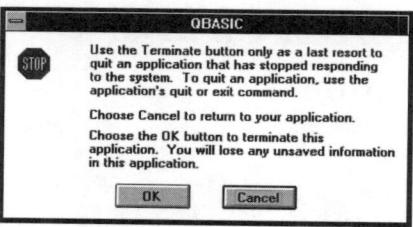

3. Click on the OK button in the Warning dialog box to terminate the application.

Notes

If your application is full-screen, Alt-Enter should place it in a window. This gives you access to the Control menu box. Otherwise, use Alt-spacebar to get access to the Control menu box.

Terminating an application is less damaging in Windows NT than in Windows 3.1. You cannot do damage to the underlying operating system by terminating an application in Windows NT, as you can with Windows 3.1 running under DOS.

Part Four:

Mastering Key Windows NT Tools

Windows NT Tools

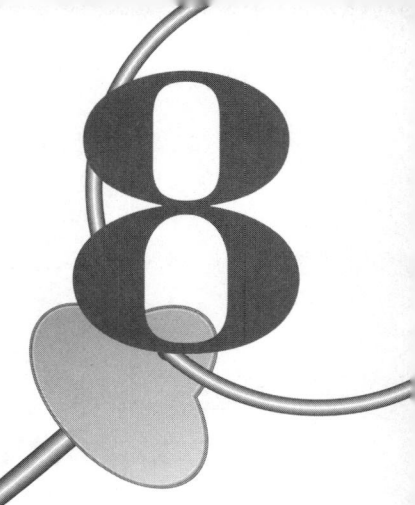

Windows NT Tools

This chapter covers the use of Windows NT tools that you can use to perform common tasks. You learn to use the built-in Clipboard that enables cutting, copying, and pasting operations; to use the Help system; and to use several utility programs that come with Windows NT.

The information is organized into the following tasks:

- Using the ClipBook Viewer
- Copying and pasting
- Cutting-and-pasting
- Creating DDE hot links
- Adding annotations to Help screens
- Removing annotations from Help screens
- Placing bookmarks in Help files
- Removing bookmarks from Help files
- Associating a file with an application

- Using the character map to insert characters in a document

- Using the Packager to edit and insert objects

- Using the Volume Control

Using the ClipBook Viewer

When To Use

Use the ClipBook Viewer to view the contents of the Clipboard and to save its contents to a permanent file. The Clipboard format is a unique format that you can access only from within the ClipBook Viewer.

Steps To Follow

1. From the Program Manager window, open the Main group by double-clicking on its group icon.

2. Double-click on the ClipBook Viewer program item icon.

3. View the current contents of the Clipboard; or take further action by using the **F**ile, **E**dit, **S**ecurity, or **V**iew menus.

Notes

The display formats that are available within the
Clipboard are those supported by the source application. When you paste information into a different
application, some of its formatting can be lost if the
same format is not supported.

Color graphics are stored in the Clipboard, based on
the capabilities of the screen driver installed in Windows NT. If you move a Clipboard file between computer systems with different display drivers, the colors
may not map properly. For this reason, transfer the file
in the original application's format (or an exported
format, such as TIFF or PCX).

The Windows NT ClipBook Viewer displays two
document windows. The first serves as the Clipboard
viewer that is familiar from Windows 3.1. This window
displays the current contents of the Clipboard, and
enables you to save the contents to a file.

The other document window serves as the *ClipBook*. In
addition to saving the Clipboard contents to a file,
ClipBook Viewer enables you to save the contents of
the Clipboard into a ClipBook, which is like a set of
Clipboards.

The ClipBook is organized into a set of pages, each
page of which functions to hold the contents of a
single Clipboard. To place information from the
Clipboard onto a ClipBook page, make sure that the
Local ClipBook document window has the focus. Select
the **P**aste option from the **E**dit menu. The Paste dialog
box appears, asking you to enter a name for the page.
Enter the name and click on the OK button. An icon
for that page appears in the Local ClipBook window
followed by the name of the page. Double-click on the
icon to see the contents of the page.

The contents of the Clipboard and the ClipBook can
be shared across a network easily. You can use the
Connect command on the **F**ile menu to connect to
another computer, and the **S**hare command on the

File menu to initiate the sharing of information. As a result, you can cut-and-paste across network connections, have DDE conversations across networks, and embed objects across the network.

NOTE
When you connect to another computer's ClipBook, ClipBook Viewer displays additional ClipBook document windows.

Copying and Pasting
When To Use
Use the Copy and Paste commands on a window's Edit menu to copy information from one application to another.

Steps To Follow

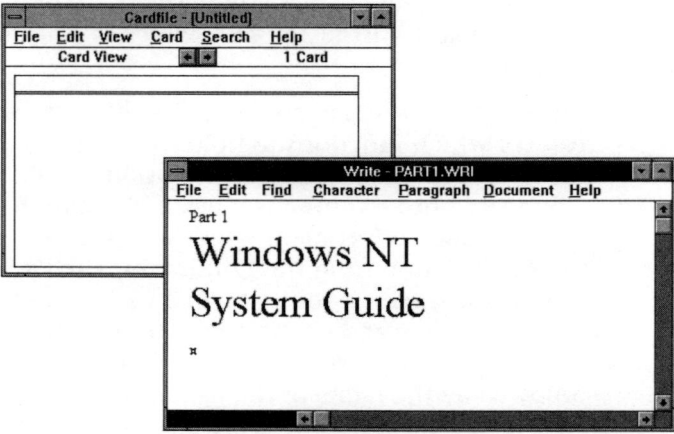

1. Open the source and destination windows.

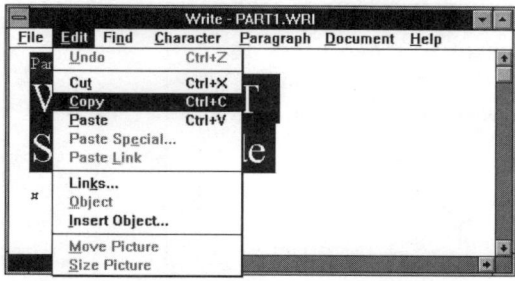

2. In the source window, select the text to be copied;
then click on the **E**dit menu, and choose **C**opy.

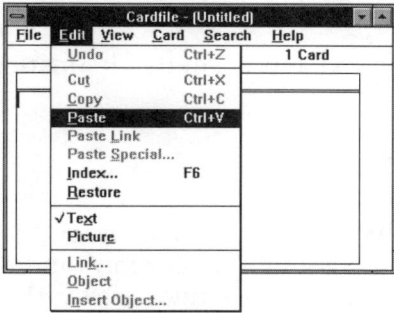

3. In the destination window, click on the **E**dit menu,
and choose **P**aste. The text appears at the current
position of the insertion point. (In Paintbrush, it
appears in the upper left corner; you drag it to the
position you want.)

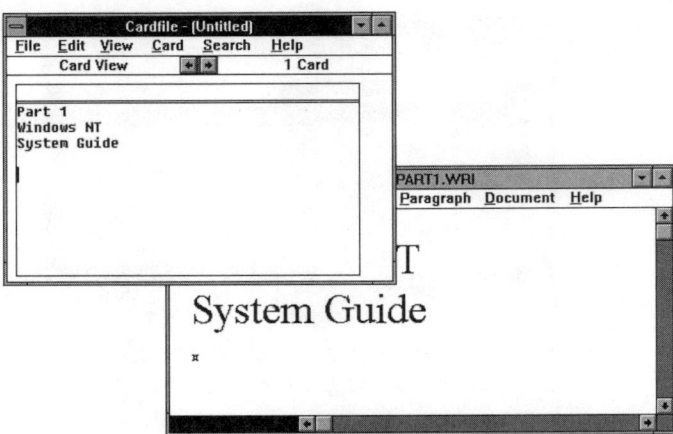

4. Verify that the text appears in the destination window.

Notes

You can use the copy and paste operation to copy information within a single application window, as well as between application windows, even though the Clipboard is not a visible function of the cut-and-paste option that is performed within software applications.

If you need to paste information from the Clipboard in a special format, select the Paste **S**pecial option from the **E**dit menu. It becomes active if it is possible to paste with a special format.

Cutting-and-Pasting
When To Use

Use the Cu**t** and **P**aste commands on a window's **E**dit menu to remove information from one application and place it in another application.

Steps To Follow

1. Select the area to be cut (in this example, the area containing the word Speed).

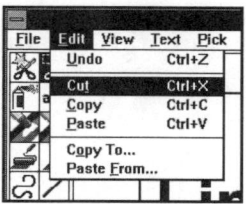

2. Click on the **E**dit menu, and choose the Cu**t** option.

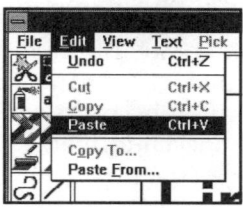

3. Click on the **E**dit menu, and choose the **P**aste option. A copy of the selected area appears in the

upper left corner. (In applications other than Paint-brush, the copy of the selected area is pasted in at the current position of the insertion point.)

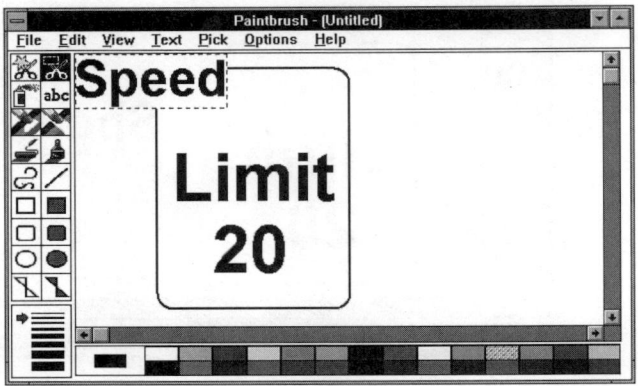

4. Drag the copy of the selected area to the position where you want to paste it. (In other applications, in which the copy of the selected area is inserted at the insertion point, this operation is unnecessary.)

5. Repeat the cut-and-paste operation until all elements are relocated.

Notes

You can use the cut-and-paste operation to move information between application windows, as well as within application windows.

If you need to paste information from the Clipboard in a special format, choose the Paste **S**pecial option from the **E**dit menu. It becomes active if it is possible to paste with a special format.

Creating DDE Hot Links

When To Use

Use the dynamic data exchange (DDE) feature to exchange data between two applications via *dynamic links*, which are advanced mechanisms for the automatic exchange of information between programs.

You can use this dynamic data exchange to link information in applications that support this feature. You can link spreadsheet data to a word-processing document, for instance. As you modify the data in the spreadsheet, the corresponding data in the word processor document reflects the changes.

Steps To Follow

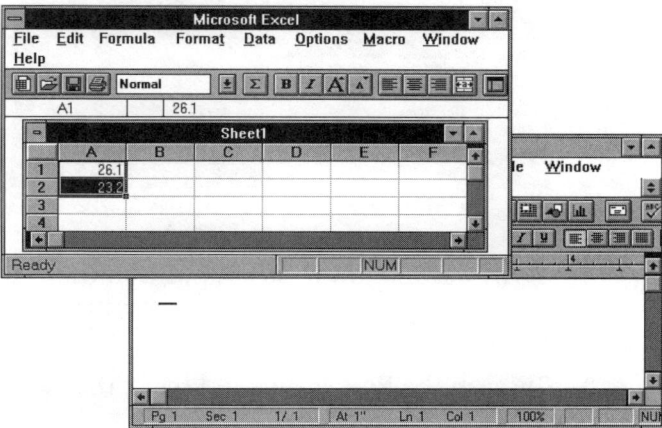

1. Open the source and destination application windows, and select the information to be linked.

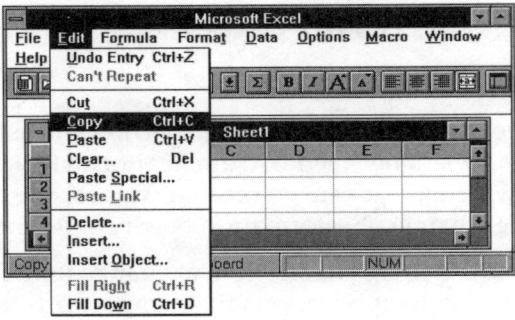

2. Click on the **E**dit menu, and choose **C**opy from the source window.

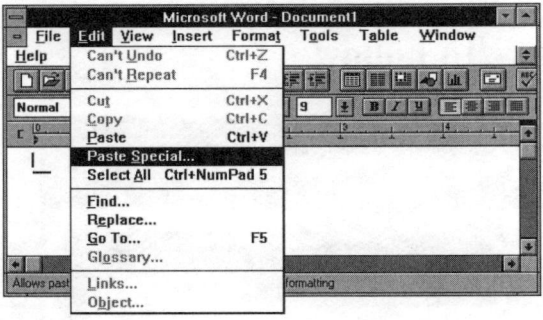

3. In the destination window, position the cursor where you want the exchange information to appear.

4. Click on the **E**dit menu, and select the Paste **S**pecial option.

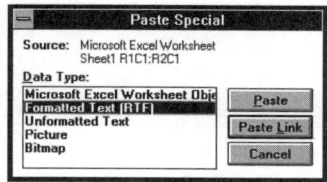

5. After the Paste Special dialog box appears, select the way you want the Clipboard to format the data before it is pasted into your document.

6. Confirm that the source data appears in the destination window.

7. You can save and close the source and destination applications, and retain the link because the hot link has been established. When you return to work, click on the icon for the application.

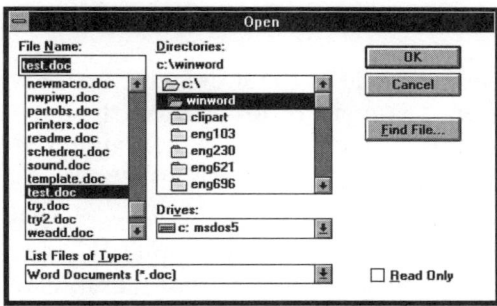

8. Click on the **O**pen option in the **F**ile menu, and select the destination document.

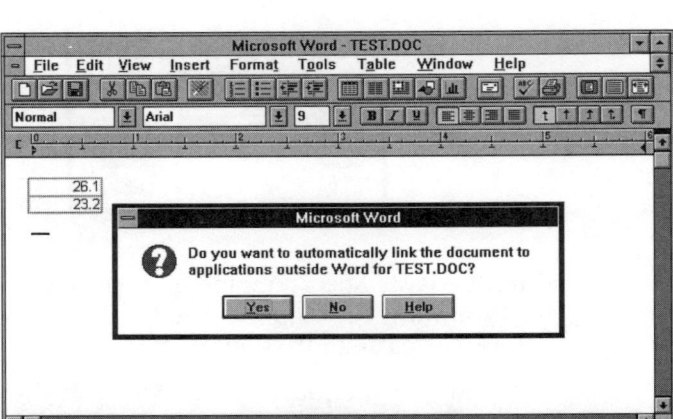

9. After the Open dialog box appears, click on the **Y**es button to confirm that Windows NT should start external automatic links.

10. If the source application is not running, Windows NT starts the source application, re-establishes the link, updates the information, and exits the source application.

Notes

If changes are made to the source document when the destination document is not opened, the application notifies the user of changes to the original the next time the destination document is opened.

In addition to creating documents that contain links to original material from other applications, you can use DDE to produce programs that manipulate information. Instead of being a distinct programming language, the DDE features are part of the application macro language; the actual commands differ between applications.

Creating DDE macros is discussed in detail in *Inside Windows 3.1* and *Maximizing Windows 3.1*, available from New Riders Publishing. (The principles of DDE remain the same in both Windows NT and Windows 3.1.)

If you want to create a DDE link between two applications, both applications must be designed to use DDE links, and you must have enough memory for both applications to run simultaneously. Because Windows NT also uses your hard drive as virtual memory, it is unlikely that you will run out of memory as you use Windows NT applications.

You cannot create DDE links with DOS-based applications.

Adding Annotations to Help Screens

When To Use

Add annotations to Help screens to customize Help files for your needs. Annotations can supplement the Help information or provide you with reminders.

Steps To Follow

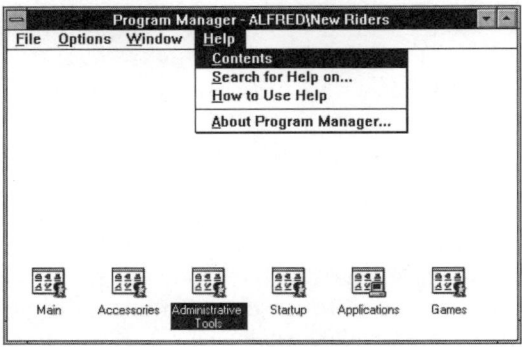

1. In any application, click on the **H**elp menu and select the type of help you want.

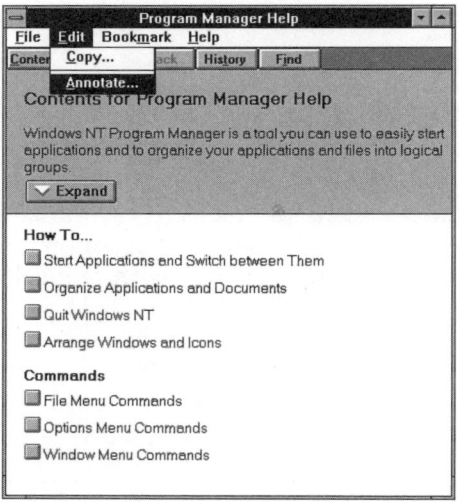

2. In the Help window, click on the **E**dit menu, and select the **A**nnotate option.

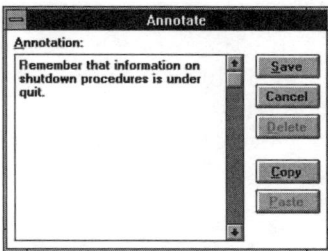

3. In the Annotate dialog box, enter the text you want to insert as an annotation, then click on the **S**ave button.

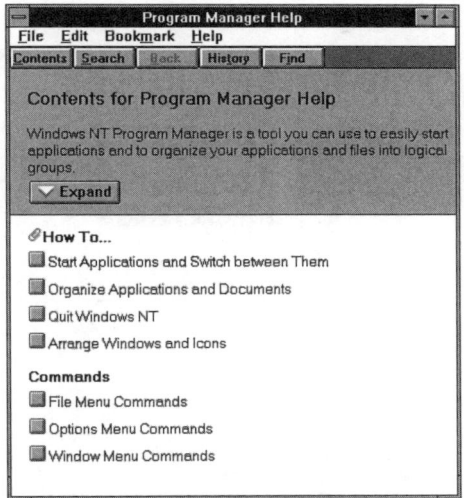

4. To view the annotation in the text, position the mouse pointer on the paper-clip icon next to the section heading, and click on the icon.

Notes

The basic text for a Help file is created in a standard word processor that can store information in Rich Text Format (RTF). The hypertext-link information is inserted as a series of footnotes within the text file.

To create an actual Help file, you need the Microsoft Help Compiler, which is available as a stand-alone product or as a part of the Microsoft Win32 Software Development Kit for Windows NT.

Removing Annotations from Help Screens

When To Use

Remove annotations from Help screens when they are no longer useful.

Steps To Follow

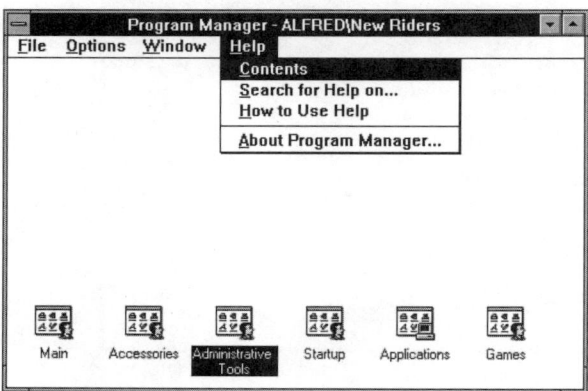

1. Click on the **H**elp menu in the application whose help you have annotated, and select the kind of help you have annotated. Move to the topic you have annotated. (These topics have paper-clip icons by the section headings.)

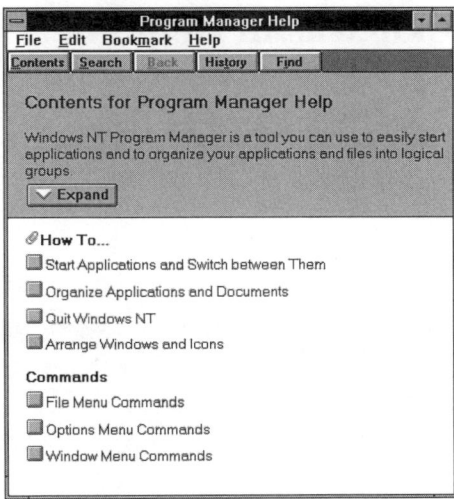

2. Click on the paper-clip icon to activate the Help Annotation dialog box.

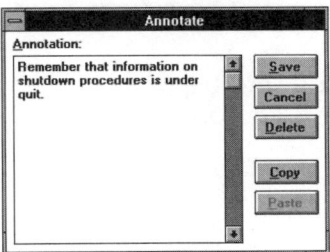

3. Click on the **D**elete button to remove the annotation.

Note

You can use the **C**opy and **P**aste buttons in the Help Annotation dialog box to copy the contents of the text box to the Clipboard or to paste the contents of the Clipboard into the text box.

Placing Bookmarks in Help Files

When To Use

Place *bookmarks* in Help files if you want to quickly return to a particular place in the Help file.

Steps To Follow

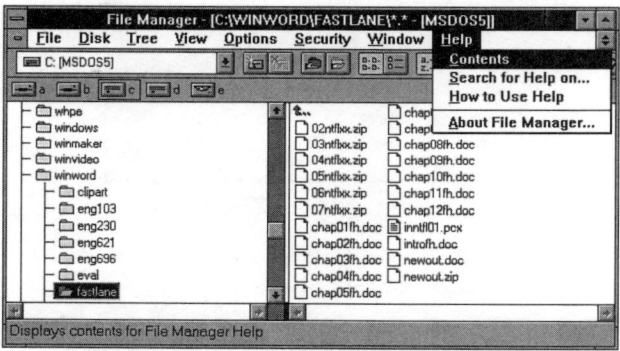

1. Click on the **H**elp menu for the application that interests you, and select the type of help you want.

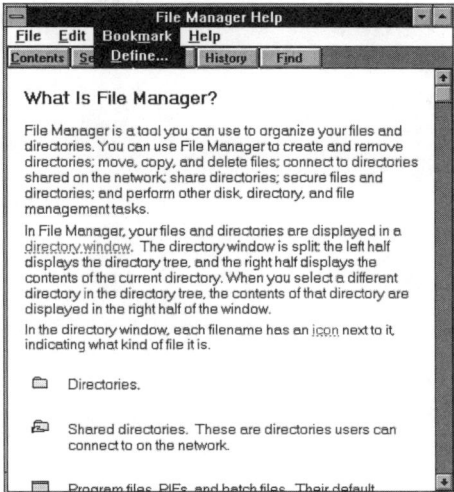

2. To place a bookmark in the file, click on the Book-**m**ark menu, and select the **D**efine option.

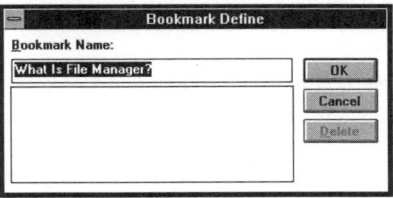

3. In the Bookmark Define dialog box, click on the OK button. The section heading for that Help topic is added to the Book**m**ark menu so that you can return to your place—simply click on the Book**m**ark menu and select your bookmark.

Removing Bookmarks from Help Files

When To Use

Remove bookmarks from Help files when they are no longer useful to you.

7 Keys to Learning Windows NT

Steps To Follow

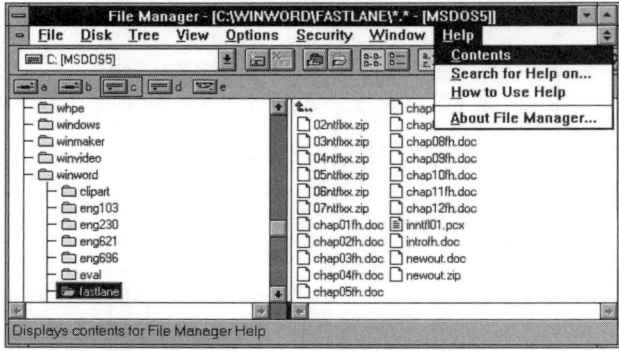

1. Click on the **H**elp menu for the application that interests you, and select the type of help you want.

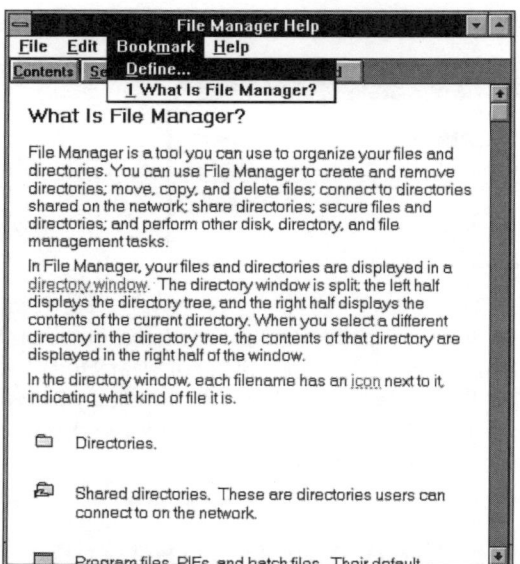

2. If you want to remove a bookmark, click on the Book**m**ark menu, and select the **D**efine option. In the Bookmark Define dialog box, click on the bookmark you want to delete in the list box.

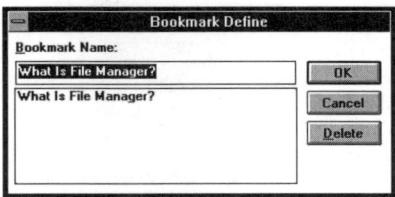

3. Click on the **D**elete button. The bookmark is removed from the Book**m**ark menu and from the
Help file.

Associating a File with an Application

When To Use

Associate a file type with an application if you want to
start the application, by double-clicking on a file of
this type in the File Manager display. The application
automatically loads and opens the file you have
associated with it.

Steps To Follow

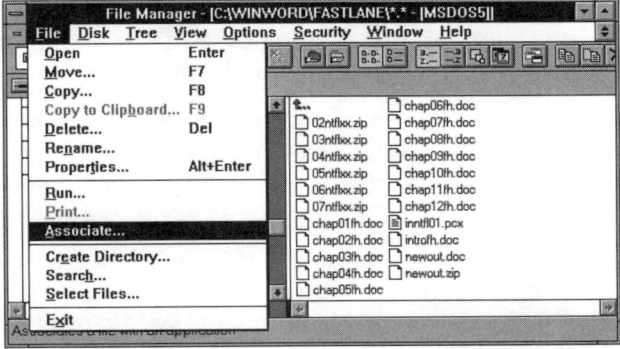

1. In File Manager, click on the **F**ile menu, and select
the **A**ssociate option.

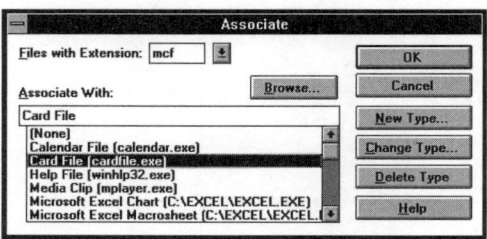

2. Type the three-letter file extension into the **F**iles with Extension text box.

3. Click on one of the applications that appears in the list box, or use the **B**rowse button to activate a dialog box that enables you to search for the application you want.

4. Click on the OK button; the file is associated with the application. When you double-click on a file with that extension in File Manager, the associated application starts and the file loads.

Notes

To clear an association, type the association in the **F**iles with Extension text box, and click on [None] in the list box. Click on the OK button, and the association clears (that is, clicking on a file with that extension no longer starts the application).

Use the **N**ew Type button to define the characteristic action that is associated with double-clicking on an associated file as opening the file or printing the file.

You can also use this dialog box to define whether the application uses DDE conversations in processing the file. (For instance, Excel documents send a DDE message to Excel requesting that the system open the document.)

Using the Character Map To Insert Characters into a Document

When To Use

Use the Character Map application to list all possible nonkeyboard characters and insert them into an application.

Steps To Follow

1. In the Program Manager, double-click on the Accessories group icon to open the group document window.

2. Start the Character Map by double-clicking on its program item icon.

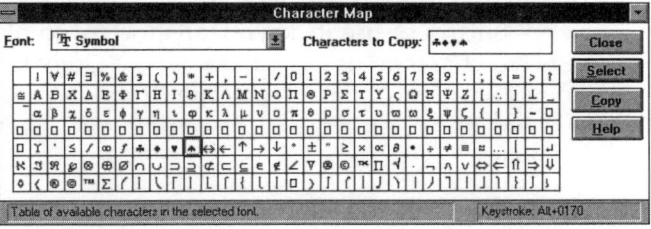

3. In the Character Map dialog box, use the **F**ont list box to select the font from which you want to select special characters.

4. Double-click on any character displayed on the character table to copy it to the Characters to Copy text box.

5. Click on the **C**opy button to copy the characters to the Clipboard.

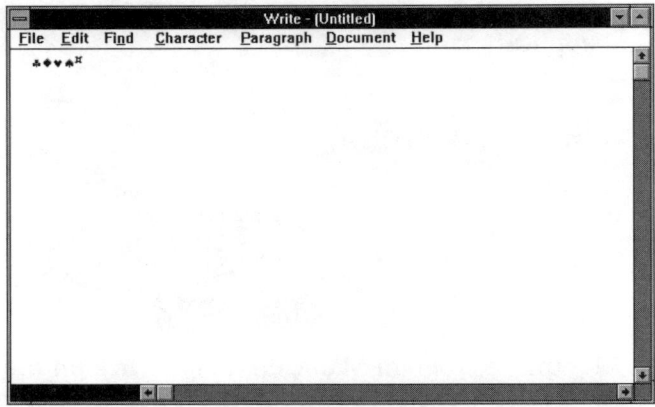

6. Click on the **E**dit menu in the application into which you want to insert the characters and choose the **P**aste option.

Notes

You may prefer to use the Tab key to move the focus to the character map and the arrow keys to move the highlighter around the map. In this case, click on the **S**elect button or use its keyboard shortcut to place the selected character in the Characters to Copy text box. You can add any character to the Characters to Copy text box by pressing the corresponding key on the keyboard.

Using the Packager
To Edit and Insert Objects

When To Use

Use the Packager to insert data objects into an application. An *object* is any item of data that an application has created. The Packager enables you to insert texts, sounds, graphics, and other types of data objects into an application's data file, even though the application cannot create that type of data. This capability, called *object linking and embedding (OLE)*, enables you to insert pictures and graphs into a word-processing document, for example, and to edit such data objects by double-clicking on them.

Steps To Follow

1. In the Program Manager, double-click on the Accessories group icon to open the group document windows.

2. Double-click on the Object Packager program item icon.

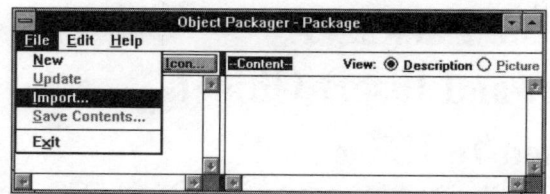

3. In the Object Packager—Package dialog box, click on the **F**ile menu, and select the **I**mport option.

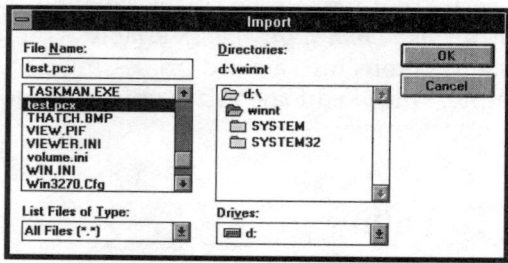

4. In the Import dialog box, click on the file name of the object you want to embed. (You can select a Paintbrush picture, an Excel spreadsheet document, or Word document, for instance.) Click on the OK button.

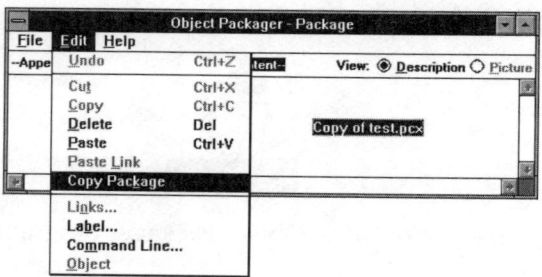

5. Click on the **E**dit menu, and choose the Copy Pac**k**age option. The object you have imported is pasted onto the Clipboard.

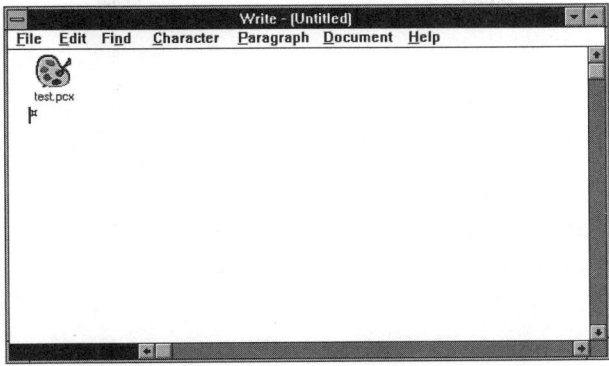

6. In the application into which you want to insert the object, click on the **E**dit menu, and choose the **P**aste option. The object is pasted into your document.

Notes

Windows NT may not set up the Packager in a Program Manager group. If you cannot find the icon, use File Manager, and double-click on PACKAGER.EXE in the \WINNT\SYSTEM32 directory.

Applications, such as Object Packager, that create objects are called *server applications*. Applications that can accept objects are called *client applications*. Not all applications can function as client applications. As object linking and embedding technology grows in popularity, however, more and more applications will be able to accept objects.

Cardfile, Paintbrush, Sound Recorder, and Write can function as client or server applications in this version of Windows NT. Cardfile and Write can serve as both.

If you want to package only part of a document (a few

cells of a spreadsheet, for instance) as an object, open the application that created the document, and copy the information you want to package to the Clipboard. Open the Object Packager, and paste the information into the Content window. Then proceed from step 5. The application that created the partial document must function as a server application, and the application that receives the object must function as a client application.

You can insert documents created by server applications directly into client applications by using the mouse. Open the File Manager, and drag the document to the client application. Press Shift-Ctrl, and drop the document into the client application.

If you want to run a program or a batch file from within a document, you can package a command line as an object. Click on the Object Packager's **E**dit menu, and select the Co**mm**and Line option. Type the command line you want in the text box, and click on the OK button. Click on the **I**nsert Icon button to select an icon, and proceed from step 5.

Double-click on the object to edit it. The application that created it starts and loads the object so that you can make changes.

Objects can contain DDE links to the application that created or packaged them. The Paste **L**ink option on the Object Packager's **E**dit menu enables you to create a link between the document and the Object Packager. After this link is created, double-click on the object to edit its contents. This not only starts the application that created the document, but also starts the Object Packager so that you can update its packaging.

Some applications come with several object-packaging applications. Microsoft Word for Windows NT comes with Equation Editor to insert mathematical equations, Microsoft Draw to insert pictures, Word Art to insert graphics made with text, and Microsoft Graph to insert graphs and charts. All of these applications work the same way that Object Packager does.

Using the Volume Control

When To Use

Use the Volume Control application to adjust the volume of Windows NT's sounds. You must have a sound card for this procedure.

Steps To Follow

1. In the Program Manager, open the Accessories group by double-clicking on its icon.

2. Open the Volume Control by double-clicking on its icon.

3. Adjust the slider control to adjust the sound volume.

Notes

If you want to temporarily mute Windows NT sounds, use the **M**ute button in the Volume Control.

If you want to adjust the volume for individual channels on your sound card, use the **E**xpanded View
option on the Control menu to show the individual
channel controls.

Part Five:
Managing Files

File Manager

File and Disk Management

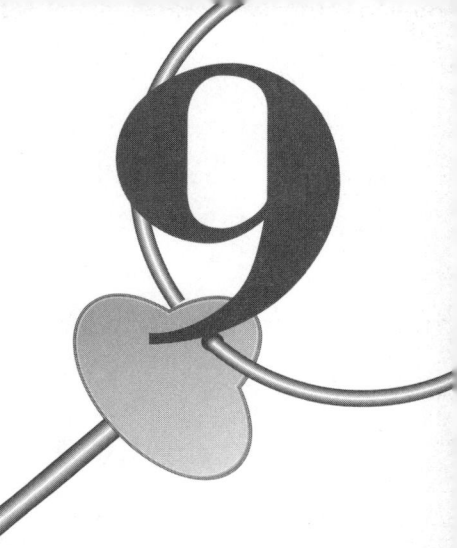

File Manager

This chapter discusses the File Manager utility. In this chapter, you learn to start the File Manager, to adjust the view of your files and directories, to sort files, and to select files.

The information is organized into the following tasks:

- Opening the File Manager
- Opening a directory window
- Indicating expandable branches
- Expanding the directory tree
- Collapsing a branch
- Including files in the directory window
- Selecting files
- Selecting the view of the directory tree and files
- Adjusting the split between the directory tree and the directory contents
- Viewing file information

- Sorting file information
- Refreshing the File Manager screen
- Navigating the File Manager
- Navigating the directory tree
- Customizing the File Manager's look

Opening the File Manager
When To Use

Open the File Manager utility if you want to copy, move, rename, or delete files. You can also perform directory operations such as creating, copying, and moving subdirectories from the File Manager.

The File Manager application window always contains at least one document window called a directory window. The *directory window* is split between a window that displays a visual representation of the directories on a disk (a *directory tree*) and a window that displays a list of the contents (files and subdirectories) of the directory highlighted in the directory tree window.

Steps To Follow

1. From the Program Manager window, open the Main group by double-clicking on its icon.

2. Double-click on the File Manager program item
   icon.

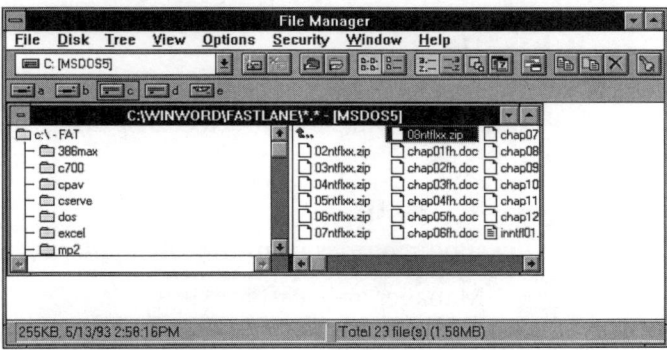

3. Double-click on a *folder* icon, which represents a
   DOS directory, to view the contents. Click on a *drive*
   icon to change drives.

Notes

Every time you open the File Manager, the contents of
the entire disk must be scanned to create the directory
tree. If you use the File Manager regularly, do not close
the application. When the File Manager is minimized,
it stores the information about the disk contents; it
does not have to reread the disk to display the information.

Windows applications automatically notify the File
Manager of any changes that they make to the file
structure. Some file actions that you take, however,
might not force an update of the File Manager directory window.

You can use the **R**efresh option on the **W**indow menu (or press F5) to update a File Manager directory window at any time.

Opening a Directory Window
When To Use

Open a directory window any time you want to view the contents of multiple directories or drives.

Steps To Follow

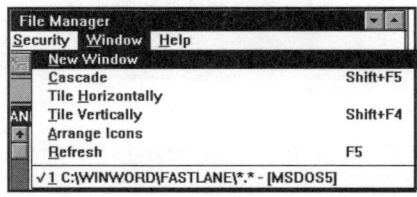

1. In the File Manager window, click on the **W**indow menu, and select the **N**ew Window option.

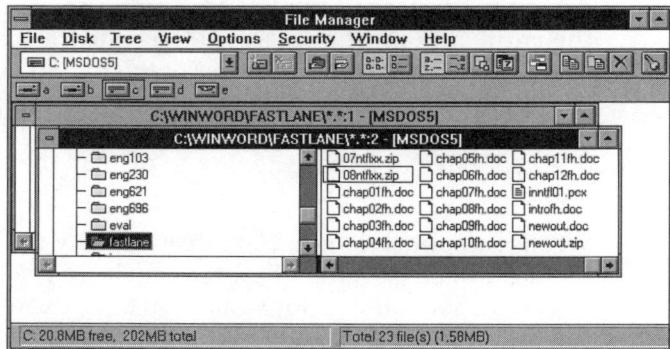

2. Select the drive you want to view by clicking once on the drive icon, and then choose the directory you want to view by clicking once on the directory icon. (After the new directory window is created, it is an exact copy of the directory window that was previously highlighted.)

Notes

To open a new directory window, you can double-click on the drive icon for the drive whose information you want to display.

Indicating Expandable Branches

When To Use

Use this option to learn which directories contain subdirectories.

Steps To Follow

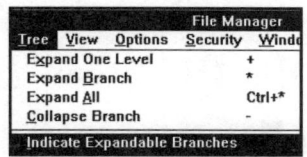

1. In the File Manager window, click on the **T**ree menu, and choose the **I**ndicate Expandable Branches option.

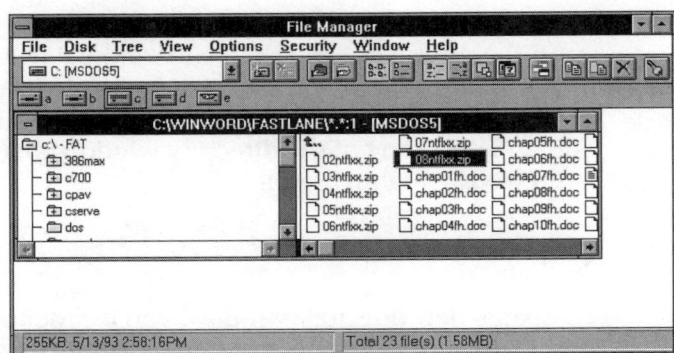

2. The branches that contain subdirectories show plus (+) signs in their icons; they change to minus (–) signs if you expand the directory icons by double-clicking on them.

Notes

To turn off this feature, repeat the preceding steps.

Leave **I**ndicate Expandable Branches turned off to improve the speed of the File Manager.

Expanding the Directory Tree

When To Use

Expand the directory tree to see the subdirectories available to you.

Steps To Follow

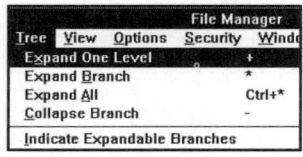

1. In the File Manager window, click on the **T**ree menu.

2. Choose the E**x**pand One Level option to show the group of subdirectories that branch from the highlighted parent subdirectory.

3. Choose the Expand **B**ranch option to show all the subdirectories that branch from the highlighted parent subdirectory.

4. Choose the Expand **A**ll option to display every branch in the subdirectory tree.

Notes

You can expand any subdirectory one level by double-clicking on it. You can collapse any expanded subdirectory by double-clicking on it. Directories that have several levels can be completely collapsed by double-clicking on the leftmost parent in the tree.

Press + to expand the highlighted directory one level. Press Shift-* to completely expand the highlighted branch. When the root directory is highlighted, press Shift-* to expand all subdirectories in the tree. The arrow keys move the highlight up and down the directory tree.

Collapsing a Branch

When To Use

Collapse a branch of the directory tree if you no longer need to see the contents of the lower-branching subdirectories.

Steps To Follow

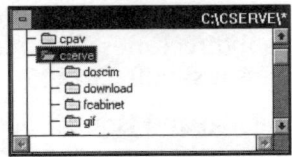

1. Click on the parent directory of the branch you want to collapse.

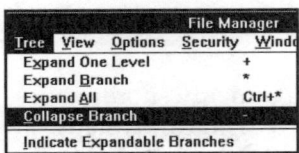

2. Click on the **T**ree menu, and choose the **C**ollapse Branch option. (**C**ollapse Branch takes action only on the highlighted subdirectory in the directory window.)

Notes

Press – or double-click on any expanded subdirectory to collapse it.

You can collapse the root directory to clear the directory-window display of all subdirectories, and then expand one level to view the first-level subdirectories. (This action returns you to the same view you saw when the directory window was opened for the first time.)

Including Files in the Directory Window

When To Use

Use the By File **T**ype command to decide which files to include in the directory contents.

Steps To Follow

1. In the File Manager window, click on the directory window whose contents you want to affect.

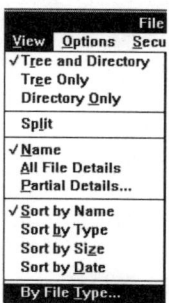

2. Click on the **V**iew menu, and select the By File **T**ype option.

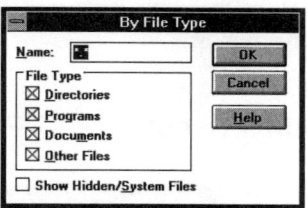

3. In the By File Type dialog box, select the file types you want to display by clicking on the appropriate check boxes or by entering a new file specification in the **N**ame text box.

4. Click on the OK button.

Notes

Enter file names and extensions in the **N**ame text box
to select files with matching names. You can use wild
cards as part of the specification. To display only those
files with an HLP extension, for example, enter ***.HLP**
in the **N**ame text box.

Selecting Files

When To Use

Use the mouse with the Shift and Ctrl keys to select
files on which the File Manager will take action.

Steps To Follow

Single Files

Click on the file name in the directory contents to
select it for action.

Contiguous Group

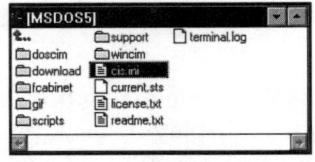

1. Click on the starting file as you would a single file.

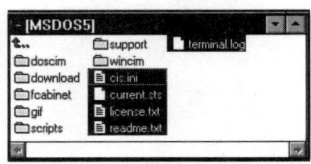

2. Hold the Shift key down, and click on the ending file. All files within the range are selected.

Non-Contiguous Group

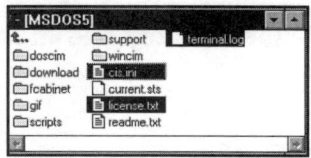

Hold the Ctrl key down, and click on the files you want to add or remove from the highlighted group.

Notes

Use the **V**iew menu to organize files so that the files are sorted in a manner you want.

See "Viewing File Information" in this chapter for more information.

Rather than highlighting files individually, it can be easier to select an entire group of files, and then deselect unwanted files from the group by holding down Ctrl and clicking on the unwanted files.

You can also select files by using the **S**elect Files option on the **F**ile menu. Choosing this option brings up a dialog box that enables you to select files by entering a file specification with wild-card characters, such as ***.HLP**. If it is more convenient to select files of a particular type by using wild cards, choose this option.

Selecting the View of the Directory Tree and Files

When To Use

Use the first section of the **V**iew menu to determine how you see the directory tree and the directory contents.

Steps To Follow

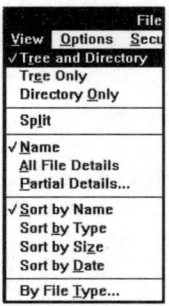

1. Click on a directory window in the File Manager window. Click on the **V**iew menu.

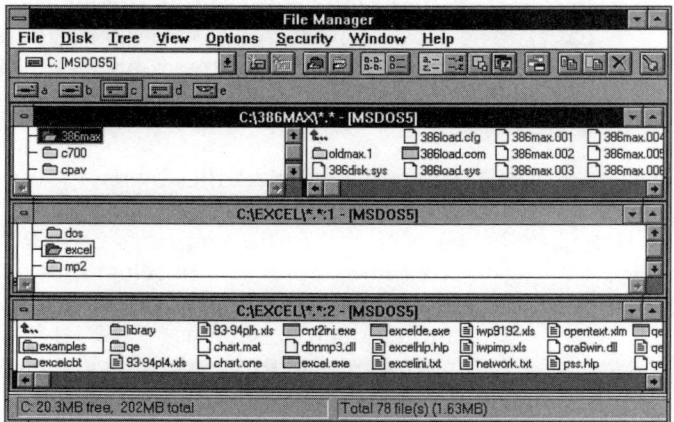

2. Click on T**r**ee and Directory to see both the directory tree and directory contents. Click on Tr**e**e Only
   to see only the directory tree. Click on Directory
   Only to see only the directory contents.

Adjusting the Split
Between the Directory Tree
and the Directory Contents
When To Use

Use this option to resize the windows for the tree and
directory display by adjusting the split between the
directory tree and the directory.

Steps To Follow

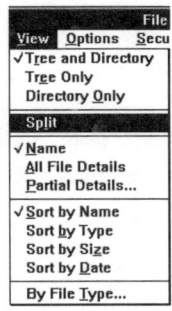

1. Click on the **V**iew menu, and select the Sp**l**it option.

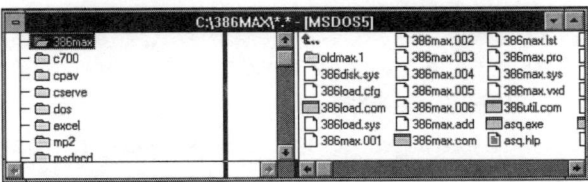

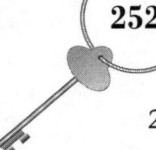

2. Roll the mouse until the split line is where you want it; Click at this new location to make the new position permanent.

Notes

As a shortcut, position the mouse pointer at the split line between the directory tree and the directory contents. Notice that the mouse pointer changes to indicate a change in the window size. Drag the split line to readjust its position.

Viewing File Information
When To Use

Use the third section of the **V**iew menu to determine what file information you view in the directory contents.

Steps To Follow

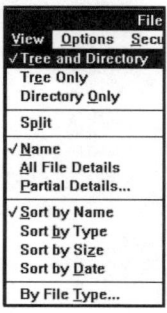

1. In the File Manager window, click on the **V**iew menu.

2. Choose the **N**ame option to see only file names.

3. Choose the **A**ll File Details to see all the file information.

4. Select the **P**artial Details option to select which details you want to see.

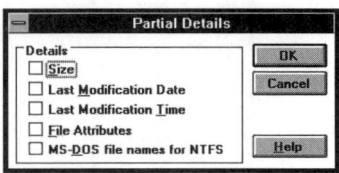

5. In the Partial Details dialog box, check the boxes that represent the file details you want to see. Then click on the OK button.

Notes

Arrange files by type if you want to copy a group of files with the same extension.

For more information on copying files and directories, see Chapter 8.

Arrange files by name if you want to copy a group of files with the same root name.

Sorting File Information
When To Use

Use the fourth section of the **V**iew menu to sort files by the file information that DOS maintains to organize the information displayed in the directory contents.

Steps To Follow

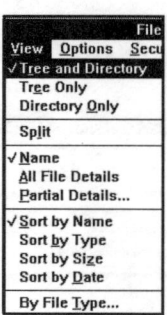

1. In the File Manager window, click on the **V**iew menu.

2. Choose the **S**ort by Name option to sort the files by name alphabetically.

3. Choose the Sort **b**y Type option to sort the files by extension.

4. Choose the Sort by Si**z**e option to sort the files by size.

5. Choose the Sort by **D**ate option to sort files by date.

Notes

The date that is maintained for a file is the most recent modification date—it is updated whenever there is a change to the contents of the file. Copying, moving, and renaming do not change the modification date. If you plan to use the date feature, make sure you set the system date and time.

For information on setting the date and time, see Chapter 5.

Refreshing the File Manager Screen

When To Use

Refresh the File Manager screen any time you think that a program may have modified a file or directory, and the change does not yet appear on the File Manager screen.

Steps To Follow

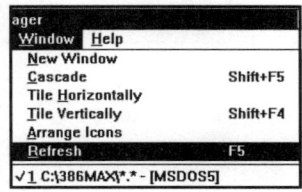

1. Click on the File Manager's **W**indow menu.
2. Choose the **R**efresh option.

Notes

The F5 key performs the same action as the **R**efresh option.

Navigating the File Manager

When To Use

Read this section to learn to navigate among multiple directory windows and among multiple drives in the File Manager.

Steps To Follow

1. If you have multiple directory windows open, you
   can switch windows by clicking on the window you
   want to become active, or by pressing Ctrl-Tab or
   Ctrl-F6.

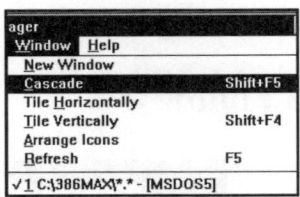

2. Use the Tile **H**orizontally, **T**ile Vertically, and
   Cascade options on the **W**indow menu to arrange
   multiple directory windows so that you can see
   them easily.

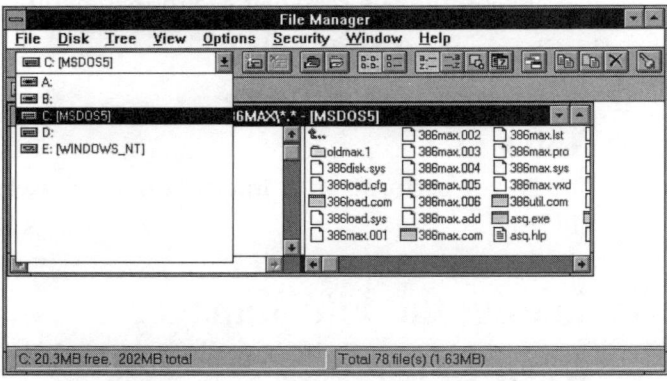

3. To change drives in a directory window, click on the
   drive icon, and press Ctrl as you press the drive
   letter from the keyboard; or use the drop-down list
   box on the toolbar.

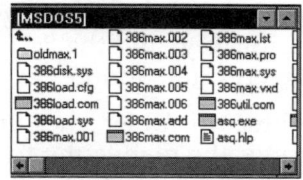

4. Use the scroll bar to scroll through a long list of directory contents. (The arrow keys and the PgUp and PgDn keys perform the same action.)

5. Click on the directory tree window or the directory contents window to make it active. You can also use the Tab key to move the focus between the directory tree window, the directory contents window, and the drive icon.

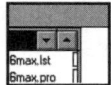

6. Use the minimize and maximize buttons on directory windows to reduce the number of directory windows visible or to make a single directory window occupy the entire workspace.

Navigating the Directory Tree

When To Use

Read this section to learn how to navigate the directory tree effectively.

Steps To Follow

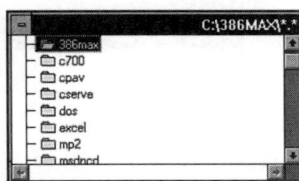

1. Use the scroll bars to scroll through a long directory tree. (The arrow keys and the PgUp and PgDn keys also perform this function.)

2. To open a directory folder, click on the directory folder, or move the highlighter to it with the arrow keys or the PgUp and PgDn keys.

3. Double-click on a directory folder to expand or collapse the directory branch one level. (Press Enter when the highlighter is on the directory folder to accomplish the same task. You can also use the commands on the **T**ree menu.)

4. Double-click on the up-directory icon to move up to the parent directory. (Press Enter when the up-directory icon is highlighted to accomplish the same task.)

Customizing the File Manager's Look

When To Use

Use the commands on the **O**ptions menu to customize the look of the File Manager to suit your working style.

Steps To Follow

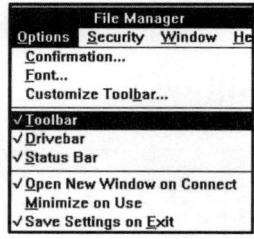

1. From the File Manager, click on the **O**ptions menu.

2. Use the menu options in the second section to control whether the **T**oolbar, **D**rivebar, and **S**tatus Bar are displayed.

3. Use the menu options in the third section to control whether settings are saved on exit, whether the File Manager minimizes after you use it, and whether a new directory window is opened when you connect to a drive on another computer.

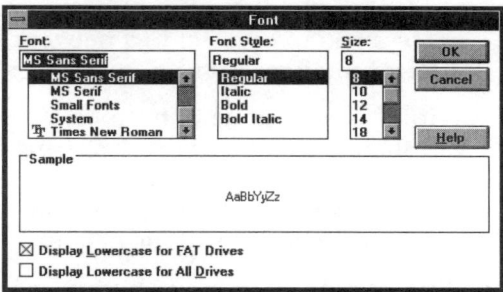

4. Use the **F**ont option to open a dialog box that enables you to select the font that the File Manager uses. Select the font information in the combination boxes, and click on the OK button. You can use the check boxes to control whether uppercase is used to distinguish between drives that use FAT and other file systems.

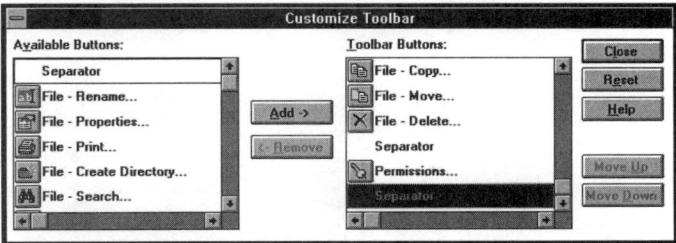

5. Use the Customize Tool**b**ar option to open a dialog box that enables you to add and remove buttons from the toolbar. Highlight the buttons you want

to add or remove in the list boxes, and use the buttons to do so. Use the Move **U**p and Move **D**own buttons to change the position of one of the toolbar buttons. Use the R**e**set button to restore the toolbar to its default state.

TIP

The Windows NT File Manager has a toolbar that places several frequently used commands on buttons. Starting on the left, the first group of buttons enables you to connect to a network drive or to disconnect.

With the next group of buttons, you can share a directory or stop sharing it. The third group enables you to adjust the view between showing only file names and showing all file details.

With the fourth group of buttons, you can determine how files are sorted: by name, by type, by size, or by date. The next button opens a new directory window. The next group on the right, a group of three, enables you to copy, move, or delete a file. With the final button, you can set file permissions.

File and Disk Management

This chapter shows you how to use the File Manager to manage your files and disks. You learn to label, format, and copy floppy disks; to select a drive; and to copy, delete, move, and rename files. You also learn to set file attributes, create directories, manage network-drive connections, and deal with file-security options under the Windows NT file system.

The information is organized into the following tasks:

- Labeling a disk
- Formatting a floppy disk
- Copying a floppy disk
- Selecting a drive
- Opening a file or directory
- Copying files and directories
- Deleting a file or directory

- Moving a file
- Renaming a file
- Confirming file actions
- Printing a file
- Setting file attributes or properties
- Creating associations
- Creating a directory
- Searching for a file
- Establishing a network connection
- Removing a network connection
- Setting file or directory permissions
- Auditing file or directory use
- Taking ownership of files or directories

Labeling a Disk

When To Use

Use this option to add a volume label to a floppy disk.

Steps To Follow

1. Select the disk you want to label by clicking on its icon.

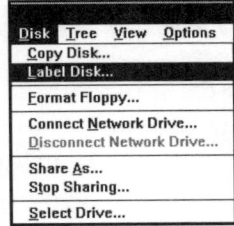

2. Click on the **D**isk menu, and choose **L**abel Disk.

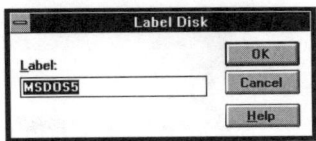

3. In the Label Disk dialog box, enter the label for the floppy disk in the text box, and click on OK.

The label must contain 11 or fewer characters, and must not contain any spaces or punctuation marks for FAT and HPFS drives. NTFS drives may have labels that contain 32 characters.

Notes

Use *disk labels* to identify the contents of a floppy disk or the operating system used on a hard drive. (You may want to name the owner of the hard drive in the label for security reasons.) Disk labels appear on the drive bar of the directory window and in the drop-down list box on the toolbar.

Formatting a Floppy Disk

When To Use

Use this option to prepare a floppy disk for use in the DOS or Windows NT environment.

Steps To Follow

1. Insert a floppy disk in the drive.

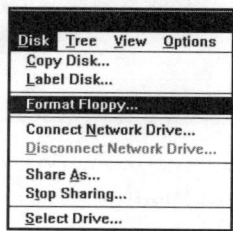

2. Click on the **D**isk menu, and choose **F**ormat Floppy.

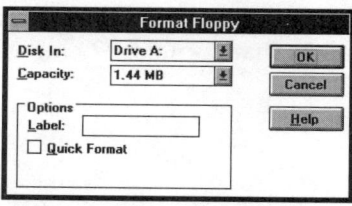

3. Specify the drive and density in the Format Floppy dialog box, and then click on OK.

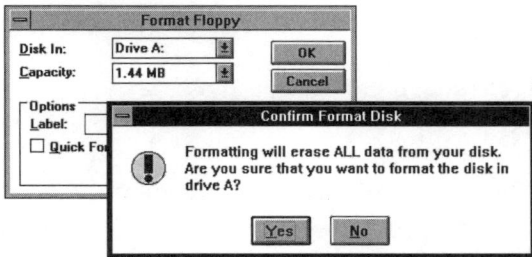

4. Click on **Y**es in the confirmation box that appears. (To cancel the operation, click on Cancel.)

Notes

To add a disk label when you format, type up to 11 characters (FAT and HPFS) or 32 characters (NTFS) in the **L**abel text box of the Format Disk dialog box.

You cannot make a system disk using Windows NT. Windows NT does not allow booting from a floppy disk for security reasons. The SYS command has been deleted from the commands you can type at the command prompt.

If your floppy disk is already formatted, you can use **Q**uick Format, which formats the disk but does not check for errors on the disk. Use **Q**uick Format only for disks that are known to be error-free. Check the **Q**uick Format box in the Format Disk dialog box to use this option.

In Windows NT, you cannot format a floppy disk by inserting it into the drive and clicking on the icon for that drive, as you can in Windows 3.1. A dialog box appears to inform you that the disk does not appear to be formatted.

Windows NT uses the FAT file system for floppy disks to ensure portability with Windows 3.1, DOS, and OS/2.

WARNING All information on a disk is destroyed when you format it.

Use **C**onfirmation in the **O**ptions menu to control whether the Confirm Format Disk dialog box appears.

Copying a Floppy Disk

When To Use

Use this feature to create a duplicate of a disk.

Steps To Follow

1. Click on the **D**isk menu, and choose **C**opy Disk.

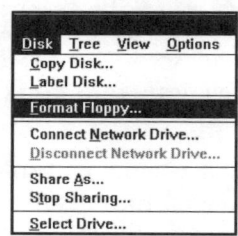

2. In the confirmation box, click on **Y**es to confirm the action.

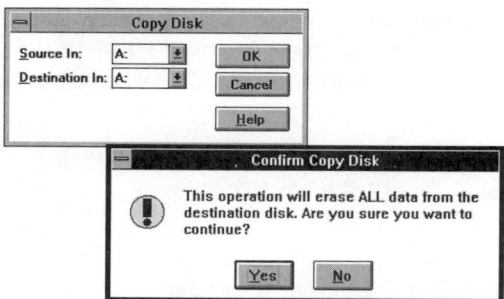

3. Follow the instructions on the screen until the copying process is complete.

Notes

If your computer has two disk drives, enter the letter of the destination drive in the dialog box that appears. (If you have only one disk drive, this dialog box does not appear.)

You can omit confirmation dialog boxes by using **C**onfirmation in the **O**ptions menu.

The disk-copying process destroys any data on the destination disk. Make certain that you have the correct destination disk and that it contains no data you want to save.

Selecting a Drive

When To Use

Use this option to choose the active disk drive for a directory window.

Steps To Follow

1. In the **D**isk menu, click on **S**elect Drive.

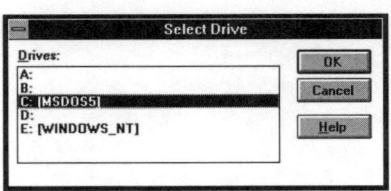

2. In the Select Drive dialog box, click on the selected drive in the list box.

3. Click on OK.

Notes

You can also select a drive by clicking on the drive icon by pressing Ctrl and the drive letter (A, C, and so on) or by using the drop-down list box on the toolbar. Double-clicking on the background of the drive bar brings up the selected drive dialog box. Only the drives that you have labeled will have names.

Opening a File or Directory
When To Use

Use the **O**pen command to open the object you have selected.

Steps To Follow

1. Select the object you want to open.

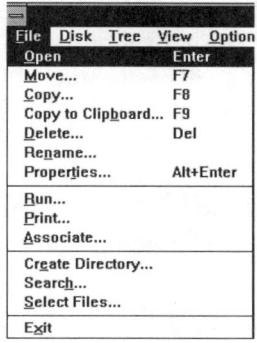

2. Click on the **F**ile menu, and select the **O**pen option.

Notes

The action that takes place is the default action for the
object you have selected. If you select a directory in
the directory tree, it expands to show its subdirectories.
If you select an executable file, it runs. If you select a
nonexecutable file, its associated application (if there is
one) opens and loads the file.

Copying Files and Directories

When To Use

This feature is used to create a duplicate of a file, a
group of files, or a subdirectory of files.

Steps To Follow

1. In the directory contents window, select the files
   you want to copy, or select the directory folder you
   want to copy. You can select directory folders from
   the directory tree or from the directory contents
   window.

2. Press and hold down Ctrl, and drag the files to the new directory folder in the directory window. Note that if you are copying files, the cursor changes into a file(s) icon and includes a plus (+) sign to indicate that the files are being duplicated.

3. In the confirmation box, confirm your mouse action by clicking on **Y**es, or cancel the copy operation by clicking on **N**o.

4. Click on OK. (To cancel the copy operation, click on Cancel.)

Notes

Before you copy the selected files, make certain that the target directory folder is visible in the directory window. If it is not visible, select **T**ree and choose Expand **A**ll, or double-click on the directory folders you want to expand.

If you select a directory folder to copy, a duplicate of the directory folder and the included files is created in the destination directory's folder.

Refer to Chapter 9 for instructions on selecting files and directories.

If you drop files on a drive icon, the files are copied to the default directory of that drive. You can also drop files into an open directory contents window to copy files to the directory whose contents are shown. In addition, you can drag-and-drop to the directory tree shown in another directory window.

Use the Confirmation option in the Options menu to turn on or off file-action confirmations. Turning off all confirmations enables you to copy, move, or delete files with your mouse without Windows NT prompting you for confirmation each step of the way.

 Be careful that you do not turn off Confirm on Replace. Without this confirmation, you can accidentally copy over a file with the same name or copy over a later version of a file with an earlier version.

You can also copy files by using the Copy option under the File menu. First, select the files, as you did in step 1 of the preceding procedure, and then click on the File menu, and choose Copy. Enter the target directory in the To dialog box. The copy button on the toolbar, the leftmost button in the group of three on the right, can speed this process.

 If the files you want to copy are located in many different directories, or if you are not certain where the files are saved, see the section on searching for files in this chapter.

Deleting a File or Directory
When To Use
Use this task when you want to permanently remove a file or directory. If you specify a directory and press Del, the entire directory, including all files and subdirectories, is deleted.

Steps To Follow

1. Select the file or files (or the directory or directories) you want to delete. To select all files, first select one file, and then press Ctrl-/.

2. Press the Del key.

3. To finish deleting the files, or to cancel the operation, respond to any confirmations presented. See the following Notes for information on customizing the confirmation options.

Notes

You can also delete files by using the **F**ile menu. Select the files you want to delete, click on the **F**ile menu, and then select **D**elete. The delete button on the toolbar, the rightmost button in the group of three on the right, can speed this process.

Use the **C**onfirmation option in the **O**ptions menu to turn on or off file-action confirmation. Turning off all confirmations enables you to delete files or directories by using your mouse without Windows NT prompting you for confirmation each step of the way. Less-experienced Windows NT users should leave the File **D**elete and D**i**rectory Delete confirmations on to prevent accidental deletion of files.

You cannot delete a file marked **R**ead Only or one that is marked as H**i**dden. See the section on setting file attributes or properties in this chapter for more information.

If the files you want to delete are located in many different directories, or if you are not certain where the files are located, see the section on searching for files in this chapter.

Moving a File

When To Use

Use this task if you want to relocate a file from one directory to another directory.

Steps To Follow

1. Select the file, group of files, or directory you want to move.

2. Drag the files to their new directory folder in the directory window. Note that because you are moving files, the cursor does not include a plus (+) sign after it changes into the file(s) icon.

3. Respond to any confirmations presented to finish moving the files or to cancel the operation.

Notes

Before you move the selected files, make certain that the target directory folder is visible in the directory window. If it is not visible, select **T**ree and choose Expand **A**ll, or double-click on the directory folders you want to expand.

You can drop files into an open directory contents window to move files to the directory whose contents are shown. You can also drag-and-drop to the directory tree shown in another directory window. If you drop files on a drive icon, the files are copied—not moved— to the default directory of that drive.

Use the **C**onfirmation option in the **O**ptions menu to turn on or off file-action confirmations. Turning off all confirmations enables you to copy, move, or delete files with your mouse without Windows NT prompting you for confirmation each step of the way.

You can also use the **M**ove option under the File menu to copy files. Select the files as you did in step 1 of the

preceding procedure, click on the **F**ile Menu, and choose **M**ove. Enter the target directory in the To dialog box. The move button on the toolbar, the center button in the group of three on the right, can speed this process.

TIP

Refer to Chapter 9 for more information on selecting files and directories.

Renaming a File

When To Use

Use this feature to change the name of a file, a group of files, or a directory within a directory window. If you select a group of files before you choose Re**n**ame, each file is presented individually for renaming.

Steps To Follow

1. Select the file, group of files, or directory you want to rename.

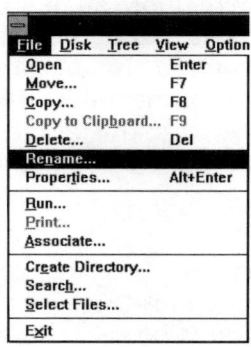

2. Click on the **F**ile menu, and choose Re**n**ame.

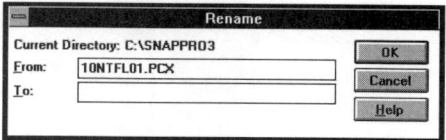

3. Enter the new file name. If you are renaming a group of files, you can use wild cards in the new name, or you can enter each file's new name as the dialog boxes appear.

4. Click on OK.

Notes

Use **M**ove in the **F**ile menu to rename a file and move it from one directory to another in a single step.

Confirming File Actions

When To Use

Use this option to determine which delete commands, replace commands, disk commands, and mouse actions you want to confirm before the File Manager completes the operation.

Steps to Follow

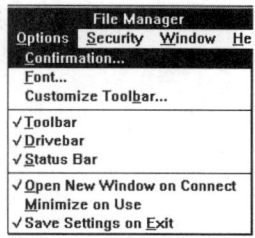

1. Click on the **O**ptions menu, and choose **C**onfirmation.

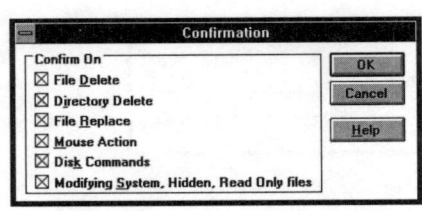

2. In the Confirmation dialog box, check or uncheck the boxes to set the confirmation options you desire.

3. Click on OK.

Notes

- Check the **M**ouse Action box to confirm move or copy actions using the mouse. This option is checked by default.

- Check the File **D**elete and Di**r**ectory Delete boxes to prevent accidental deletion of files and directories. This option is checked by default.

- Check the File **R**eplace box to prevent accidental replacement of files using the same name or replacement of older versions of files with new versions. This option is checked by default.

- Check the Dis**k** Commands box so that you do not accidentally format a disk or copy one disk over another.

- Check the Modifying **S**ystem, Hidden, Read Only files box to keep from accidentally making changes to files that are critical to the function of your system. You should probably never uncheck this box.

If you are an inexperienced Windows NT user, leave the confirmation options set to the default settings to avoid most common accidental deletions and overcopyings. If you are an experienced Windows NT user, use caution when changing the confirmation settings.

Printing a File

When To Use

Use this command to print a file that has an associated application.

Steps To Follow

1. Select the file you want to print.

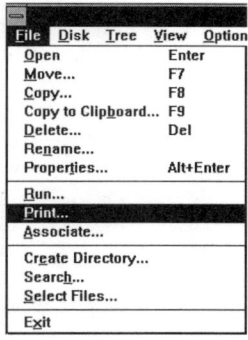

2. Choose the **P**rint option on the **F**ile menu.

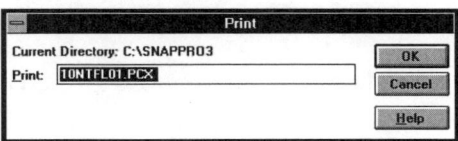

3. Respond to any print dialog box that appears. (The one that appears depends on the associated application.)

Notes

The file prints on the default printer.

If the Print Manager is running, you can print files with associated applications by dragging them from the File Manager and dropping them on the Print Manager.

Setting File Attributes or Properties

When To Use

Use this command to display and alter file attributes.

Steps To Follow

1. Select a file, a group of files, or a directory you want to change.

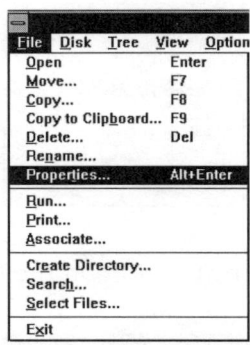

2. Click on the **F**ile menu, and choose Proper**t**ies.

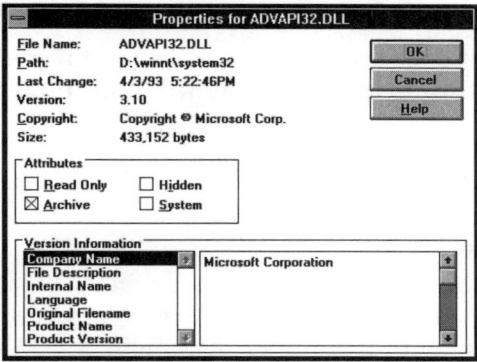

3. Check or uncheck the attributes you want to change in the Properties dialog box, and then click on OK.

Notes

File attributes are maintained by Windows NT. A check next to an attribute indicates that the attribute is active. The four attribute options are as follows:

- **R**ead Only does not permit changes to be saved to the file.

- **A**rchive marks the file as "archive" if it has changed since the last time it was backed up.

- **Hi**dden does not display the file in a standard directory.

- **S**ystem enables the operating system to use the file.

Choose **A**ll File Details in the **V**iew menu to see all file details, including attributes. Choose **P**artial Details— and check the **F**ile Attributes box—to see only the file attributes.

If a file is marked as Hi**d**den, you cannot see it in the File Manager display unless you select Show Hidden/**S**ystem Files in the By File **T**ype option in the **V**iew menu.

A file cannot be deleted if **R**ead Only is checked.

You can also set the same attributes for directories by selecting the directory and following this procedure.

Creating Associations

When To Use

Use this command to associate a document (or file) extension with the application that can manipulate the document or file. After a document is associated with an application, you can add the document as an item to a Program Manager group, and you can activate the item by double-clicking on its icon.

Steps To Follow

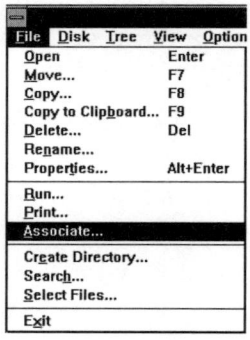

1. Click on the **F**ile menu, and choose **A**ssociate.

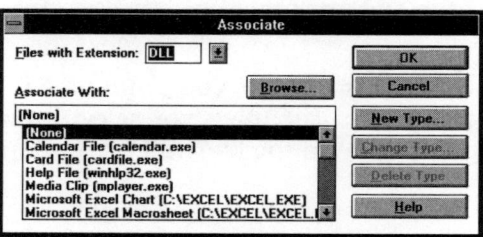

2. In the combination box, choose the application you want to associate with a file extension.

3. Enter the extension you want to associate in the drop-down list box, or select one from the list, and then click on OK.

 After a file is associated with an application, it has a document file icon (with lines that represent lines of text) next to it in the File Manager directory window.

Notes

To cancel an association, enter the file extension in the text box, and choose None from the list box.

If the application appears in the list box, not only can you open the application and load the file by double-clicking on the file name in a File Manager directory window, but you can also print the file by dragging the file name and dropping it on the Print Manager's icon. Applications that have this capability are automatically installed in the **A**ssociate With list box.

If an application does not appear in the combination box, use **B**rowse to locate it, and then build the association. If an application is not included in the combination box, you cannot use the drag-and-drop printing feature. You can use the **N**ew Type button to define the attributes and behavior of an application you want to include in the combination box. The application must take advantage of drag-and-drop features, of course.

Each document extension can be associated with only one application, but many extensions can be associated with a single application. For example, you can associate the extensions TXT and NOT to Notepad. If you change the association for a document extension, the previous association is canceled.

Any associations created for DOS applications are based on a PIF rather than the actual application file.

Creating a Directory

When To Use

Use this command to make a new subdirectory in the directory tree.

Steps To Follow

1. In the directory tree, select the directory in which you want to create the new directory.

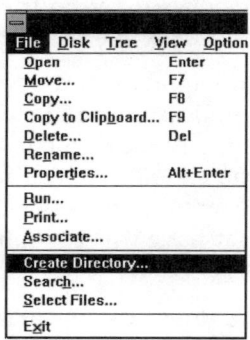

2. Click on the **F**ile menu, and choose Cr**e**ate Directory.

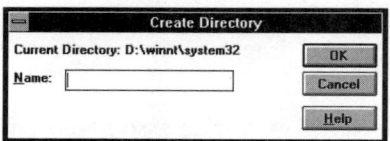

3. In the Create Directory dialog box, enter the name of the new directory, and then click on OK.

Notes

Use short names for directories so that they can easily be included in a path. You can name a directory to include an extension.

For FAT drives, the name must be eight or fewer characters in length, and contain no spaces or punctuation. For NTFS drives, the name can contain up to 256 characters.

You can create multiple levels of directories at a time by using the backspace (\) to indicate the beginning of a subdirectory.

Searching for a File

When To Use

Use this command to locate a file or group of files within a branch of the directory tree or anywhere on a disk. The complete paths for all file names that match the file specification are displayed in the Search Results window.

Steps To Follow

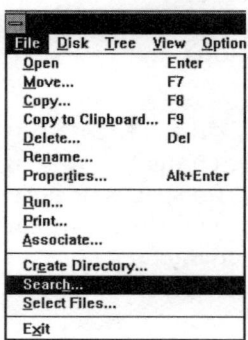

1. Click on the **F**ile menu, and choose Searc**h**.

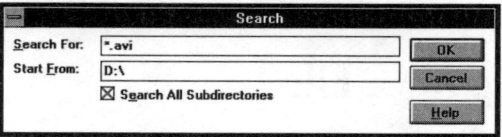

2. In the Search dialog box, enter the file specification you want to find in the **S**earch For text box.

3. In the Start **F**rom text box, enter the directory from which you want to begin searching.

4. Check the S**e**arch All Subdirectories box to search all child subdirectories of the Search **F**rom directory.

5. Click on OK.

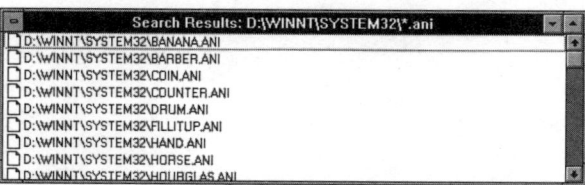

6. View the results of your search in the Search Results window. You can act on the files in this window as if they were in the directory contents area of a directory window.

Notes

Begin your search from the root directory, and check the Search All Subdirectories box to find files anywhere on your disk.

You can use the standard wild cards in the Search dialog box. The asterisk (*) represents an unknown number of characters. The question mark (?) represents a single unknown character. The file specification (*.DOC, for example), searches for all files that have the DOC extension.

The specification JAN* searches for all files that begin with the letters JAN. You cannot use the asterisk to match letters in the middle of a name. For instance, J*N searches for all files that begin with J and ignores the N. Use the question mark to create search strings for middle characters.

You can delete the files in the list by selecting them and pressing Del. You can also use the drag-and-drop feature to move files from the list to new directories. You can rename files with the Re**n**ame option in the **F**ile menu.

The **F**ile menu's Searc**h** option is useful if you want to remove unwanted BAK or TMP files that take up space on your hard drive.

Establishing a Network Connection

When To Use

Use this feature to connect to a network drive.

Steps To Follow

1. Click on the **D**isk menu, and choose Connect **N**etwork Drive.

2. Select the drive from the drive box.

3. Click on the file server or computer that appears in the list.

4. Click on the available drive to which you want to connect.

Notes

The network service must be successfully loaded before you start Windows NT in order for the File Manager to recognize any network drives.

You can move, copy, and delete files on a network drive by using the same techniques you used for moving, copying, and deleting files on your local drives.

Removing a Network Connection

When To Use

Use this feature to disconnect from a network drive.

Steps To Follow

1. Click on the **D**isk menu, and choose **D**isconnect Network Drive.

2. Click on the **B**rowse button.

3. Highlight the file server you want to detach from in the list box on the left side of the Browse Connections dialog box, and then click on the **D**etach button.

4. Click on the combination box down arrow in the Detach File Server dialog box, and highlight the file server name from which you want to detach. Click on OK.

5. Complete the operation by clicking on OK in the Browse Connections dialog box, and then click on **C**lose in the Network-Drive Connections dialog box.

Notes

Disconnecting from the network drive also disconnects you from any print queues, shared files, or applications related to that drive.

Setting File or Directory Permissions
When To Use

Set file or directory permissions to determine what level of access individual users or groups can have to the files or directories on a drive.

Steps To Follow

1. Select the file or directory for which you want to set permissions.

2. Select the **P**ermissions option on the **S**ecurity menu.

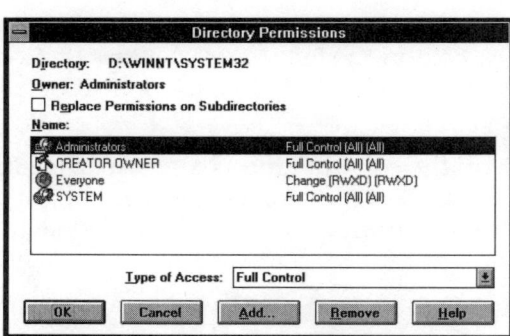

3. In the dialog box that appears, click on the **A**dd button to select to which users or groups you want to give permission.

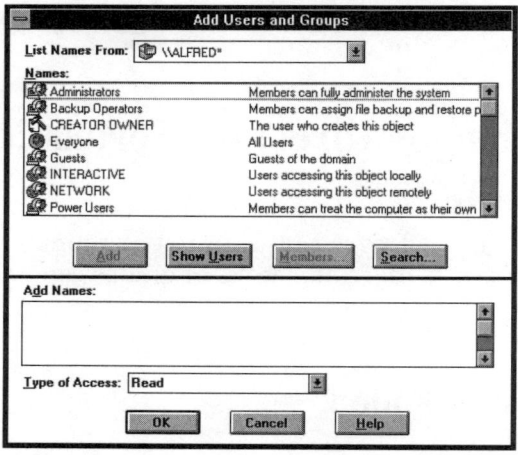

4. In the Add Users and Groups dialog box, click on the Show **U**sers button to show individual user names with the group names in the **N**ames list box. Double-click on a user or group name to add it to the A**d**d names list box (or select it and click on the **A**dd button). Use the **M**embers button to show the

individual members of a group in the <u>N</u>ames list box. Use the <u>S</u>earch button to search for a user or a group. Click on the OK button when you have completed your list of names.

5. In the Directory Permissions dialog box, select a user or group in the <u>N</u>ame list box. Use the <u>T</u>ype of Access drop-down list box to determine the type of permission you are granting. Click on the <u>R</u>emove button to remove a group or user from the list.

6. When you have finished granting permissions, click on the OK button.

Notes

You must have appropriate privileges to set permissions on files and directories.

You can grant the following types of access to users or groups:

*   **No Access**. Users have no access to the file or directory at all.

*   **List**. Users can list the contents of the directory.

*   **Read**. Users can read the contents of a file or files in a directory.

*   **Add**. Users can add files to the directory.

*   **Add & Read**. Users have a combination of the Add and Read permissions.

*   **Change**. Users can make changes to the file or directory.

*   **Full Control**. Users can have all rights to the file or directory.

*   **Special Directory Access**. Users can have any combination of the set of special permissions.

*   **Special File Access**. Users can have any combination of the set of special permissions.

The special permissions are the following:

- **Read**. Users can read the file or directory.

- **Write**. Users can write to the file or directory.

- **Execute**. Users can execute the file or files in the directory.

- **Delete**. Users can delete the file or files in the directory.

- **Change Permissions**. Users can change permissions on the file or directory.

- **Take Ownership**. Users can take ownership of the file or directory.

You can set permissions only on an NTFS drive. The permissions button on the toolbar, the one with the key icon on the right, can speed the process of setting permissions.

Auditing File or Directory Use

When To Use

Initiate file and directory auditing to keep track of which users have used a file or directory.

Steps To Follow

1. Select the directory or files you want to audit.

2. Select the **A**uditing option on the **S**ecurity menu.

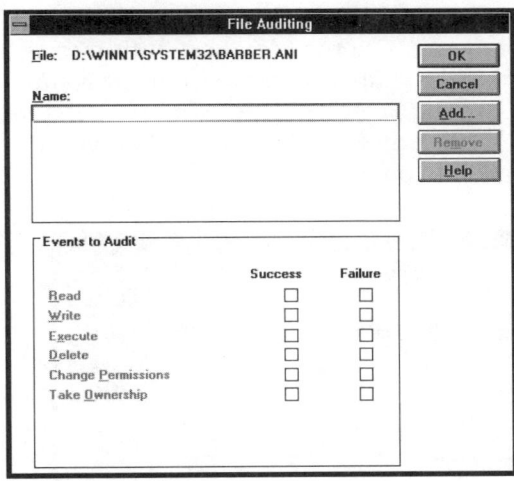

3. In the File Auditing dialog box, click on the **A**dd button to select which users or groups you want to audit.

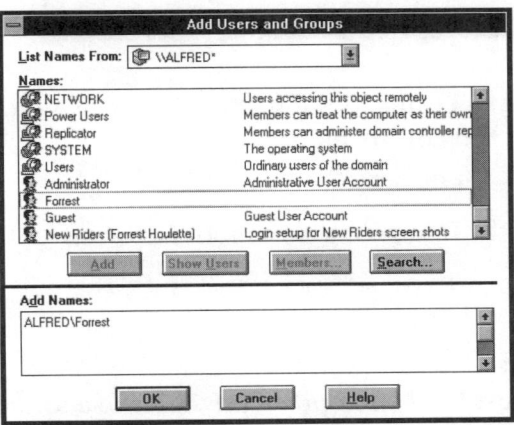

4. In the Add Users and Groups dialog box, click on the Show **U**sers button to show individual user names with the group names in the **N**ames list box. Double-click on a user or group name to add it to

the Ad**d** names list box (or select it, and click on the
Add button). Use the **M**embers button to show the
individual members of a group in the **N**ames list
box. Use the **S**earch button to search for a user or a
group. Click on the OK button when you have
completed your list of names.

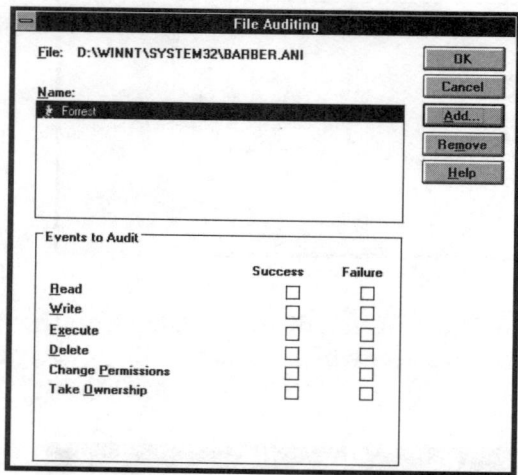

5. Use the Events to Audit check boxes to indicate
    which events to audit.

6. Click on the OK button.

7. Use the Event Viewer to monitor the log of these
    events.

Notes

You must have appropriate privileges to audit file and
directory use.

Use this feature of the NTFS file system as a way of
keeping track of who has accessed sensitive data. If
problems occur, you can determine who caused them

and which user accounts have been compromised. If
you are serious about security, be sure to monitor
failures of events as well as successes.

File and directory auditing is not available for FAT or
HPFS drives.

See the section on setting file or directory permissions in this chapter for
definitions of the events shown as
auditable in the dialog boxes.

Taking Ownership of Files or Directories

When To Use

Take ownership of files when you have disabled a
user's account, and you need to clean up before deleting the user. You can also take ownership any time
you need control of files you do not own.

Steps To Follow

1. Select the files or directories for which you want to
   take ownership.

2. Click on the **S**ecurity menu, and select the **O**wner
   option.

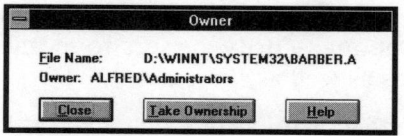

3. Click on the **T**ake Ownership button.

Notes

You must have appropriate privileges to take ownership of files, or you must have permission of the file
owner. File owners can grant permission using the
Permissions option on the **S**ecurity menu. Taking
ownership is relevant only for files on an NTFS drive.

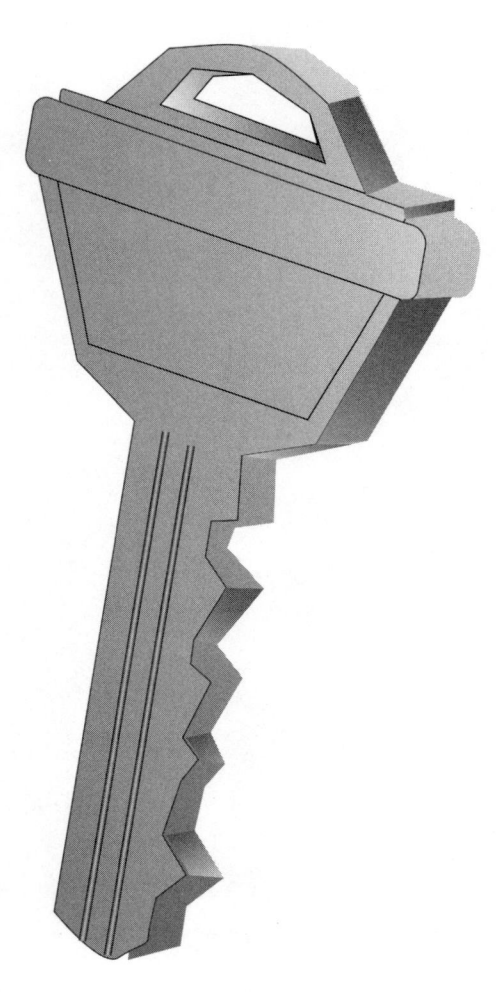

Part Six:
Printing

Printing

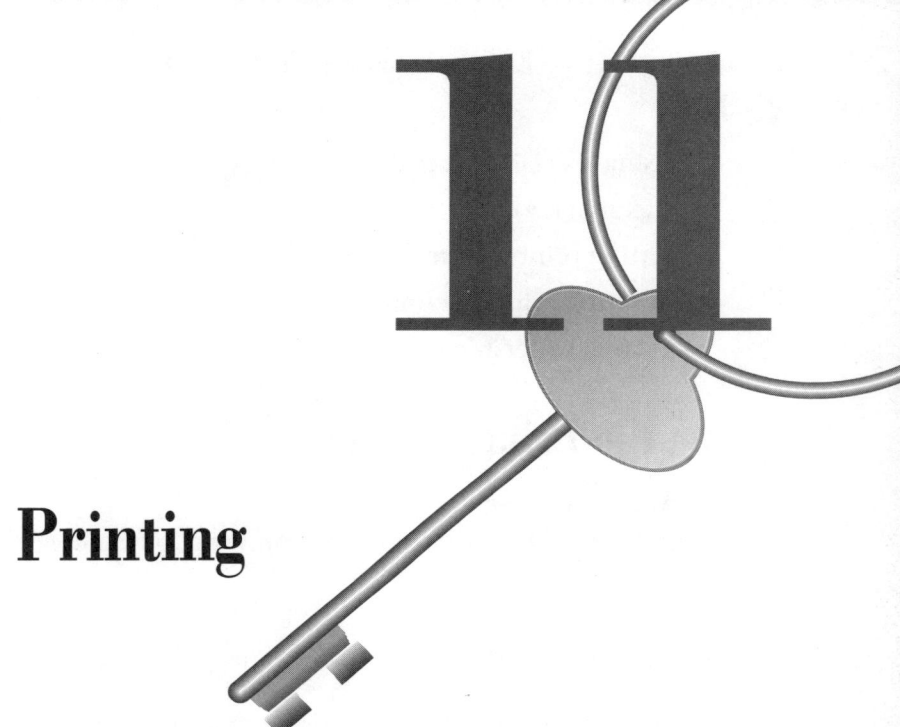

Printing

This chapter covers printing and the Print Manager. You learn to add, remove, and select printers. You also learn how to control print jobs with the Print Manager application.

The information is organized into the following tasks:

- Using the Print Manager
- Adding a printer
- Removing a printer
- Selecting a printer
- Configuring a printer
- Choosing a printer connection
- Controlling the order of print jobs
- Pausing a print job
- Resuming a print job
- Deleting a print job
- Refreshing the Print Manager screen

- Using special print features
- Creating a form
- Setting printer permissions
- Auditing printer permissions
- Taking ownership of a printer

Using the Print Manager

When To Use

Use the Print Manager to control printing jobs under Windows NT.

Steps To Follow

1. Windows NT handles printing as a background task. The Print Manager does not automatically appear as an icon when you print. If you need to start it independently of printing, open the Main group in Program Manager by double-clicking on its icon.

2. Start the Print Manager by double-clicking on its program item icon. Use the Print Manager's controls, as described in this chapter, to control your print jobs.

Notes

When you double-click on the Printers icon in the Control Panel, the Print Manager appears. Windows NT does not maintain a separate printers dialog box in the Control Panel—all issues relating to printers are handled by the Print Manager instead. The Control Panel is therefore an alternate way of starting the Print Manager.

Adding a Printer

When To Use

Use the Create Printer option on the **P**rinter menu to add a new printer to Windows NT.

Steps To Follow

1. Click on the Print Manager's **P**rinter menu, and select the Create Printer option.

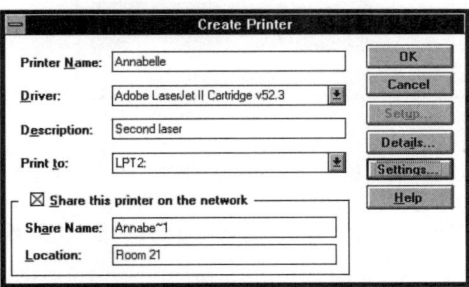

2. In the Create Printer dialog box, enter a name for the printer in the Printer **N**ame text box.

3. Select a driver for the printer in the **D**river drop-down list box.

4. Enter a description of the printer's function in the Description text box. This description informs network users of the printer's function.

5. Select the port the printer will use in the Print **t**o drop-down list box.

6. If this printer is shared on a network, check the **S**hare this printer on the network box. Windows NT then generates a compatible share name and displays it in the Sh**a**re Name text box. If you want, you can edit the share name to your liking.

7. You can also enter a description of the printer's location in the **L**ocation text box.

8. Use the Set**u**p button to configure the printer's setup. This button gives you access to features such as paper size and orientation, which may be supported by your printer's driver.

9. Use the Deta**i**ls button to determine the characteristics of your printer.

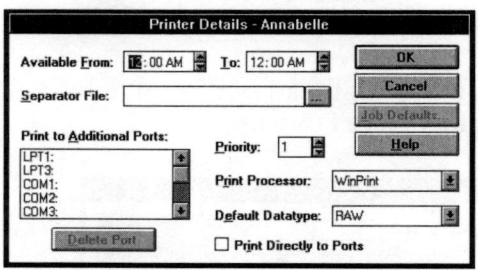

10. In the Printer Details dialog box, use the Available **F**rom and **T**o spin boxes to set the time span during which the printer will be available for printing.

11. Enter the name of a *separator file*, which prints before each print job, in the **S**eparator File text box. (The default is a page before each document.)

12. Select additional printer ports in the Print to **A**dditional Ports list box to group this printer with others

printing to those ports. (The first available printer in the group then handles the job.)

13. Use the **P**riority spin box to set the relative priority of jobs sent to the printer. Windows NT uses this value to determine the time slice devoted to printing a job on the printer.

14. Generally, you should leave the **P**rint Processor and **D**efault Datatype settings alone unless you have an application that requires them to be reset.

15. Check the Pri**n**t Directly to Ports check box if you want to bypass spooling for print jobs on this printer. (Checking this box, however, can slow your system's performance when printing takes place.)

16. Use the **J**ob Defaults buttons to specify the default settings for settings supported by your printer driver, such as paper size and orientation. Click on the OK button.

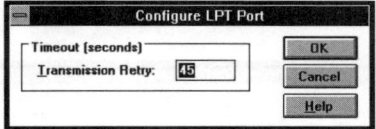

17. In the Printer Details dialog box, click on the Settin**g**s button to set the configuration for the port you have selected. The dialog box that appears depends on the port you have selected. Click on the OK button.

See Chapter 5 for more information about port settings.

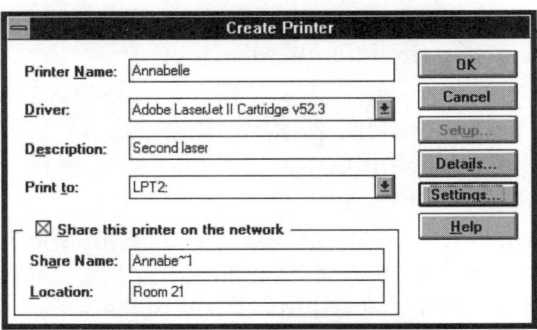

18. Click on the OK button in the Create Printer dialog box.

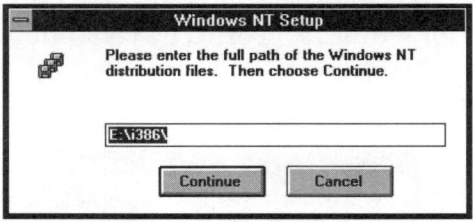

19. If no driver for your printer is installed on your system, enter the path to the disk and directory containing the drivers, put the disk or CD-ROM in the appropriate drive, and click on OK in the dialog box that appears.

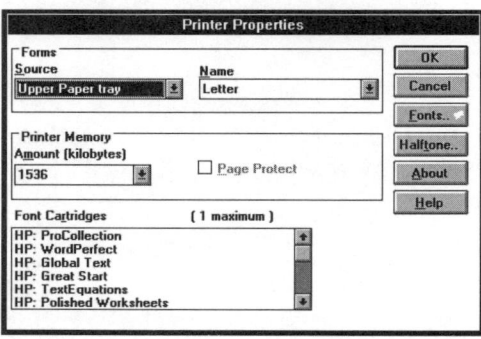

20. Set your printer's properties when the Printer
    Properties dialog box appears. The settings depend
    on the printer you are installing. Click on the OK
    button. A document window representing the
    printer appears in the Print Manager's workspace.

Notes

Use the **D**elete Port button in the Printer Details dialog
box to delete ports in the Print to **A**dditional Ports list
box that are not available on your system.

Not all the buttons described in the dialog boxes for
this procedure become active for all printers.

Use the **S**erver Viewer option on the **P**rinter menu to
create and control printers on a remote computer. You
must be logged in as Administrator or with appropriate
privileges to undertake this task.

Removing a Printer

When To Use

Use the **R**emove Printer option on the **P**rinter menu to
remove a printer from Windows NT.

Steps To Follow

1. Select the document window for the printer you
   want to remove.

2. Click on the **P**rinter menu, and select the **R**emove
   Printer option.

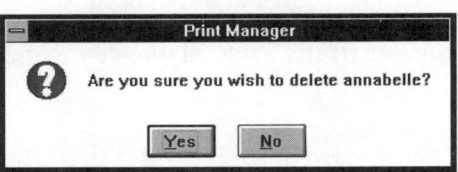

3. Click on the **Y**es button in the confirmation
   dialog box.

Notes

The **R**emove Printers operation does not delete the
printer driver from your hard drive. If you want to
reinstall the printer, repeat the Add Printers process.
You are not prompted to insert a disk in the floppy
drive because the driver is already present on the
hard drive.

To delete the driver, use the File Manager. Search
for a file ending in DLL that begins with the name
of the printer. (You should find this file in the
\WINNT\SYSTEM32\SPOOL\DRIVERS\W32X directory.)

You also can access the Printer Properties dialog box
from the Print Manager's menu. Click on the **P**rinter
menu and choose the **P**roperties option. (You can also
click on the Printer Properties button on the toolbar,
the leftmost in the group of three.)

Selecting a Printer

When To Use

Use the Printer Manager's toolbar to select your default
printer.

Steps To Follow

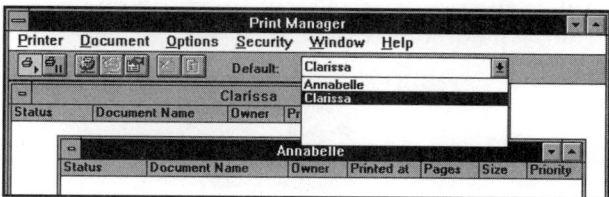

Click on the Default drop-down list box, and select a printer name.

Notes

You can install printer drivers for printers that are not physically connected to your computer by using the FILE option from the Print **t**o drop-down list in the Create Printer dialog box. You can format a document with features supported by the driver even if you do not intend to print on your system with one of the drivers. You can work on your personal system, save your work on a disk, and take the file to your work system to print. In addition, some printer drivers may enable more screen fonts than others.

Most Windows NT applications enable you to choose a printer from those installed on your system from the P**r**int Setup option of their **F**ile menu.

Configuring a Printer

When To Use

Use the **P**roperties option on the **P**rinter menu to *configure* (adjust the settings on) your chosen printer.

Steps To Follow

1. Select the printer you want to configure by clicking on its document window.

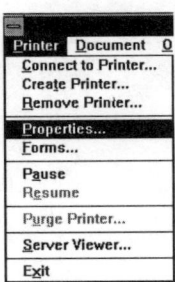

2. Select the **P**roperties option on the **P**rinter menu.

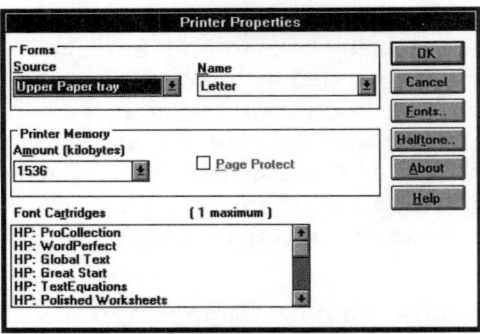

3. Use the buttons and controls in the Printer Properties dialog box to adjust the settings. The settings that are available depend on the printer you have installed.

4. Click on the OK button.

Notes

Most Windows NT applications enable you to configure a printer from those installed on your system from the P**r**int Setup option of their **F**ile menu.

Windows NT does not provide printer setup dialog boxes—the printer driver itself supplies the dialog boxes. These dialog boxes give you direct access to the way the printer driver controls the printer.

Timeout errors tell Windows NT that the target printer is not responding or is busy. Increasing the **T**ransmission Retry value increases the amount of time Windows NT will continue to try communicating with the printer before it gives you an error message. For example, an empty paper tray or a paper jam signals Windows NT that the printer is not responding correctly. Increasing the **T**ransmission Retry value causes Windows NT to wait longer before it gives you an error message (possibly until the printer can continue accepting data).

Use this option to adjust the priority associated with printing on a printer.

Choosing a Printer Connection

When To Use

Use the **C**onnect to Printer option on the **P**rinter menu to choose a network printer connection.

Steps To Follow

1. Select the **C**onnect to Printer option on the **P**rinter menu.

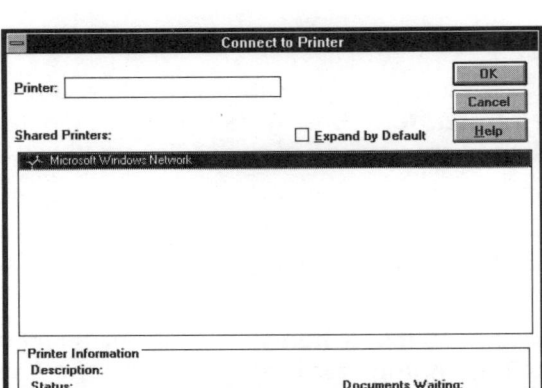

2. In the Connect to Printer dialog box, select a printer from the **S**hared Printers list box. Double-click on the names of domains or servers to see the names of printers available in them. Check the **E**xpand by Default check box to expand the list when the dialog box opens.

3. Click on the OK button.

Notes

The left two buttons in the group of three on the toolbar speed the process of connecting to and disconnecting from network printers. The left button enables you to connect; the center button disconnects you. (To disconnect from the menu, select the first option on the **P**rinter menu.)

Controlling the Order of Print Jobs

When To Use

Change the order of files queued by the Print Manager if you want a particular file to print sooner than other queued files.

Steps To Follow

1. Activate the Print Manager by double-clicking on its icon.

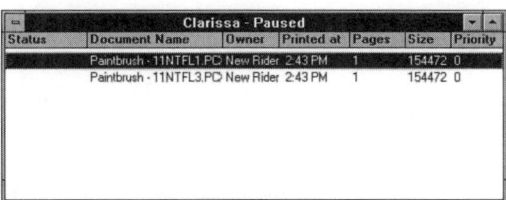

2. Select the file you want to move up in the print list by clicking on it.

3. Drag the file to its new location in the print list, and release the mouse button.

Notes

You cannot change the order of the job that is currently printing. The Ctrl-up arrow and Ctrl-down arrow keys move a print job up and down the list once the print job is selected.

You must have full-control permission on the printer to be able to change the order of print jobs.

Pausing and Resuming a Print Job

When To Use

Pause a print job if you need to free system resources devoted to printing for other application programs.

Steps To Follow

1. In the Print Manager window, click on the print job you want to pause.

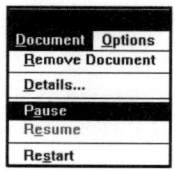

2. Click on the **P**ause option on the **D**ocument menu.

Notes

To resume a job, click on the R**e**sume option on the **D**ocument menu. You can resume print jobs after you encounter a printer problem, such as the printer running out of paper. Use the Re**s**tart button on the Document menu to restart printing from the beginning of the document.

You can also pause or resume an entire print queue by using the identical commands on the **P**rinter menu. In addition, you can use the leftmost group of buttons on the toolbar to pause and resume print jobs. The buttons adjust to pause a document or the entire printer, depending on whether you have selected a document in the printer's document window.

Deleting a Print Job

When To Use

Delete or cancel a print job to free the printer from outdated print jobs or for other purposes.

Steps To Follow

1. In the Print Manager window, click on the print job you want to delete or cancel.

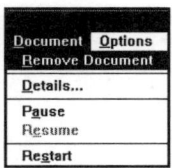

2. Click on the **R**emove Document option on the **D**ocument menu.

Notes

Use the P**u**rge Printer option on the **P**rinter menu to remove all print jobs from the selected printer's queue.

Refreshing the Print Manager Screen

When To Use

Refresh the Print Manager screen any time a print job has reached a status that is not yet reflected on the Print Manager's display.

Steps To Follow

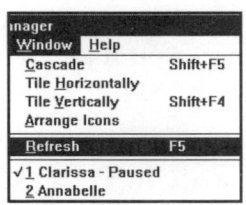

1. Click on the Print Manager's **W**indow menu.

2. Click on the **R**efresh option.

Notes

As a shortcut, you can press F5 to refresh the screen while the Print Manager is open.

Special Print Features

When To Use

Read this section to get an idea of the types of settings that Windows NT printer drivers enable you to control from the print setup dialog box.

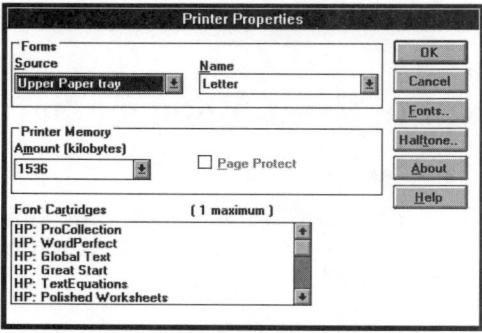

Notes

The following are typical settings that you can change with a Windows NT printer driver and the print setup dialog box:

- **Number of Copies.** Some printers handle the printing of multiple copies on their own, freeing your software for other tasks while the printer makes multiple copies. If your printer has this capability, the driver setup dialog box usually includes a text box that enables you to enter the number of copies you want to print.

- **Page Orientation.** Most printers enable you to print in *portrait* (vertical) or *landscape* (horizontal) page orientations. Printer drivers usually enable you to choose the orientation you want to use.

- **Print Resolution.** Most printers can print at a variety of resolutions, ranging from detailed high-resolution graphics to fast draft printing. This choice is usually presented as a set of option buttons.

- **Specific Printer.** Some printer drivers can be used with a set of printers, usually related models produced by the same company. As a result, when you configure the driver, you must choose the model that you have connected to your computer.

- **Paper Size.** Many printers enable you to use various paper sizes. If the printer enables you to choose a paper size, it usually presents a drop-down list box from which to make the choice.

- **Paper Source.** Many printers enable you to feed paper from several different paper trays or paper feeders. If the printer driver enables you to choose which paper source to use, it usually presents you with a drop-down list box from which to make the choice.

- **Scaling.** Many printers enable you to reduce or enlarge an image with the printer driver. This option is common on PostScript printers.

- **Options.** Many printers have specialized options that are unique to individual printer models. These options are usually set through an Options button that opens an additional dialog box. For example, these options may determine which paper bin to use, how the printer should format different types of graphic files, or if the printer should print on both sides of the page.

- **Fonts.** Many printer drivers enable you to specify resident printer fonts or soft printer fonts from the driver. This option is usually implemented as a Fonts button that opens an additional dialog box.

Creating a Form

When To Use

Create a new printer form when you find that the forms supplied with Windows NT do not match your printing needs.

Steps To Follow

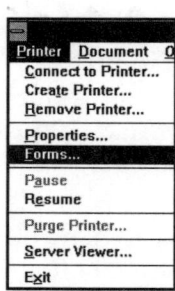

1. Click on the Print Manager's **P**rinter menu, and select the **F**orms option.

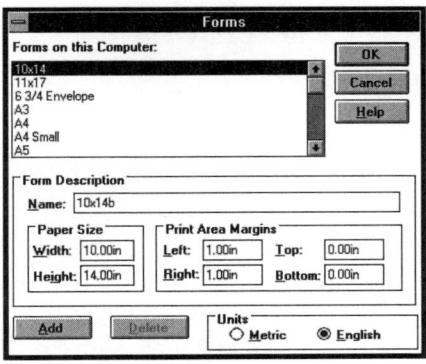

2. In the Forms dialog box, enter a name for the form in the **N**ame text box.

3. Enter appropriate settings for Paper Size and Print Area Margins. (Use the Units options buttons to determine whether you enter **M**etric or **E**nglish measurements.)

4. Click on the **A**dd button to add the form to the list of Forms on this Computer.

5. Click on the OK button.

Notes

Printer forms describe the nature of the printing medium to your printer in a standardized way.

Windows NT comes with a variety of predefined printer forms from which you can choose. You may not need to create additional forms.

Use the **D**elete button to delete a form that you no longer need. You cannot delete the Windows NT default forms.

Setting Printer Permissions

When To Use

You can set printer permissions to determine the type of access that individual users or groups have to a particular printer.

Steps To Follow

1. In the Print Manager, select the document window of the printer for which you want to set permissions.

2. Select the **P**ermissions option on the **S**ecurity menu.

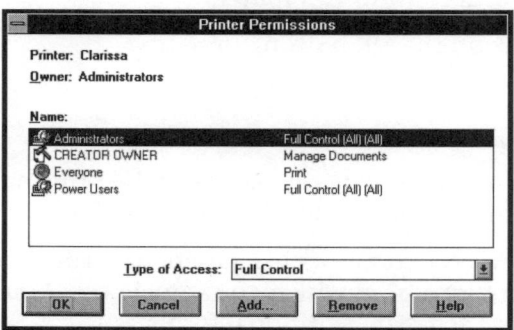

3. In the dialog box that appears, click on the **A**dd button to select the users or groups to which you are giving permission.

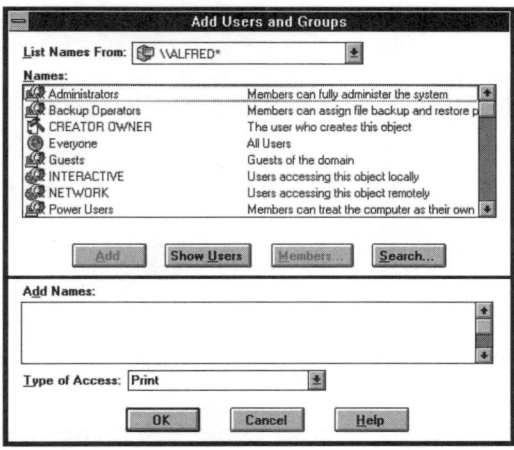

4. In the Add Users and Groups dialog box, click on the Show Users button to show individual user names and group names in the Names list box. Double-click on a user or group name to add it to the Add names dialog box (or select it and click on the Add button). Use the Members button to show the individual members of a group in the Names list box. Use the Search button to search for a user or a group. Click on the OK button when you have completed your list of names.

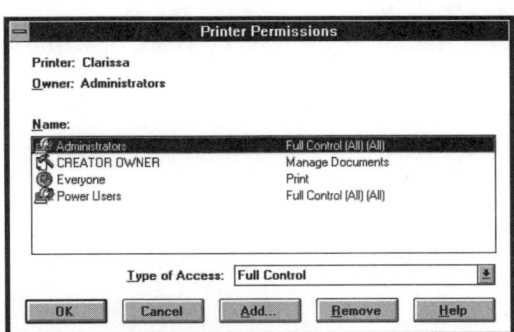

5. In the Printer Permissions dialog box, select a user or group in the **N**ame list box. Use the **T**ype of Access drop-down list box to determine the type of permission you are granting. Use the **R**emove button to remove a group or user from the list.

6. When you are done granting permissions, click on the OK button.

Notes

To set permissions on printers, you must have appropriate privileges.

You can grant the following types of access to users or groups:

- **No Access.** Users have no access to the printer.

- **Print.** Users can print on the printer.

- **Manage Documents.** Users can change the priority and delete documents from the printer.

- **Full Control.** Users have all rights to the printer.

Auditing Printer Use

When To Use

Initiate printer auditing to keep track of which users have used a printer.

Steps To Follow

1. In the Print Manager, select the printer you want to audit by clicking on its document window.

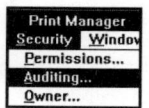

2. Select the <u>A</u>uditing option on the <u>S</u>ecurity menu.

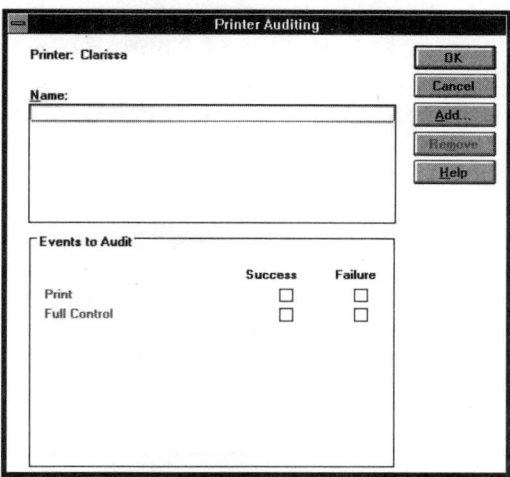

3. In the Printer Auditing dialog box, click on the <u>A</u>dd button to select which users or groups you want to audit.

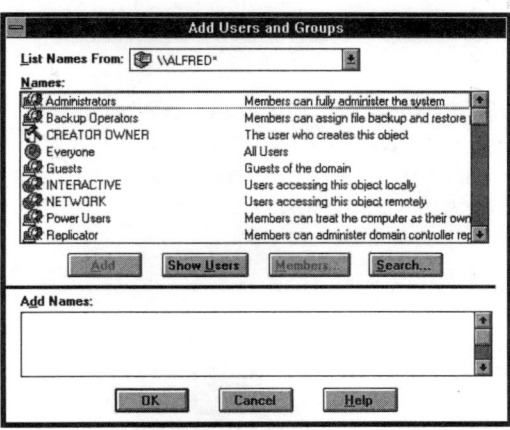

4. In the Add Users and Groups dialog box, use the Show <u>U</u>sers button to show individual user names

with the group names in the **N**ames list box.
Double-click on a user or group name to add it to
the A**d**d names list box (or select it and click on the
Add button). Use the **M**embers button to show the
individual members of a group in the **N**ames list
box. Use the **S**earch button to search for a user or a
group. Click on the OK button when you have
completed your list of names.

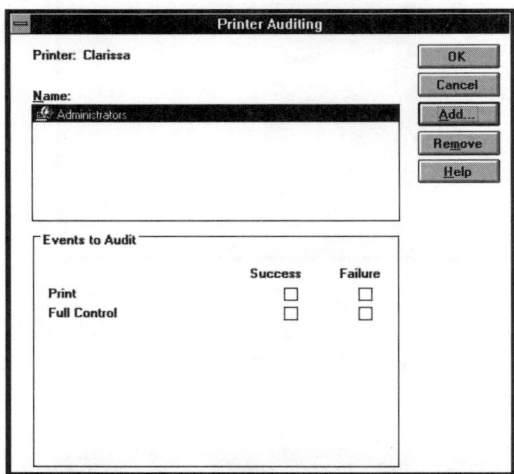

5. Use the Events to Audit check boxes to indicate
   which event to audit. The Success and Failure check
   boxes determine whether you are auditing a successfully completed action (a completed print job, for
   example) or a failed action.

6. Click on the OK button.

7. Use the Event Viewer to monitor the log of these
   events.

For more information on ways to monitor events, see Chapter 3.

Notes

You must have appropriate privileges to audit printer use.

Use this feature of Windows NT as a way of keeping track of who has printed data. If problems occur, you can determine who caused them or which user accounts have been compromised. If you are serious about security, be sure to monitor failures of events as well as successes.

See "Setting Printer Permissions" in this chapter for definitions of the events shown as auditable in the dialog boxes.

Taking Ownership of a Printer

When To Use

Take ownership of a printer when you have disabled a user's account and need to clean up before deleting the user, or any time you need control of a printer that you do not own.

Steps To Follow

1. Select the printer for which you want to take ownership by selecting its document window in the Print Manager.

2. Click on the **S**ecurity menu, and select the **O**wner option.

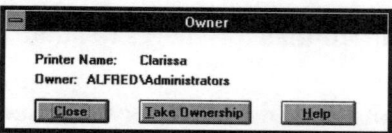

3. Click on the **T**ake Ownership button.

Notes

You must have appropriate privileges to take ownership of a printer.

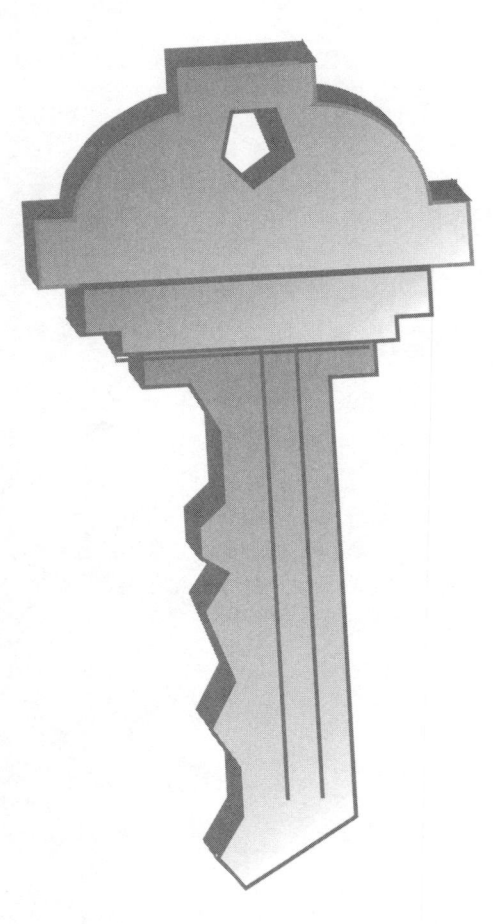

Part Seven:

Troubleshooting

Troubleshooting

Troubleshooting

This chapter covers problems that you may encounter when you install and use Windows NT.

The information is organized into these sections:

- Installation problems
- Program-performance problems
- Program Manager problems
- Printing problems
- DOS, OS/2, and POSIX applications problems

Installing Windows NT Problems

Problem: *During Windows NT installation, the system hangs or crashes.*

Steps To Follow

1. On an x86-based machine, make certain that no hardware device shares a base memory address or

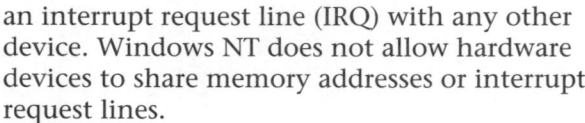

an interrupt request line (IRQ) with any other device. Windows NT does not allow hardware devices to share memory addresses or interrupt request lines.

2. Turn your printer on. Some multiple I/O cards have been known to cause a conflict between the printer port LPT1 and other devices, even though no two devices share base memory addresses or interrupt request lines. Turning the printer on usually solves this problem.

3. Reinstall Windows NT by using the Custom Setup option, which requires that you specify your hardware configuration. Check the list box for each setting to make sure that there is not a special option for your hardware.

4. If applicable, disable the autoswitching mode on the display adapter. Refer to the vendor's documentation for further information. Reboot and proceed with installation.

5. Disable ROM shadowing if your system uses it. Reboot and proceed with installation. Refer to your computer's documentation for information on ROM shadowing.

6. Disconnect any specialized peripheral devices. Reboot and proceed with installation.

7. Examine your ROM setup program for any settings that might be unique to your machine. Verify that all memory has been allocated to the microprocessor's use in some way, for instance, and that ROM setup is aware of all the peripheral devices for which it provides settings.

Notes

Because Windows NT is a new operating system, sometimes there are surprises as users install it on an ever-widening base of hardware. Before installation, review the list of compatible hardware, and make sure the machine on which you plan your installation is 100% compatible. Some hardware vendors have not yet written Windows NT device drivers.

Sometimes Windows NT mistakes an incompatible card for a card of another type. For instance, a non-SCSI CD-ROM adapter can be mistaken for a network card. If you have some incompatible hardware, and this type of problem seems to recur, remove the incompatible hardware, install Windows NT while preserving your existing operating system, and reinstall your hardware for use with the second operating system.

In addition, some hardware devices cannnot work with Windows NT in all configurations, even though the installation of their drivers takes place correctly and without errors. QIC standard tape drives, for instance, do not work when mounted externally on a dual-floppy system. You need a special cable to connect the tape drive and floppy drive B to the same connector. You should report all such problems to Microsoft Technical Support to get the latest hardware-specific information.

Problem: *There are no device drivers for my printer, display adapter, or other hardware devices included in my Windows NT package.*

Steps To Follow

1. Use a standard device driver that works for a similar device from the same manufacturer. Very often, generic drivers are compatible with a variety of specialized hardware devices.

2.   Contact your manufacturer to get a Windows NT
     device driver for your hardware. You can also
     check the Windows NT forums on bulletin board
     systems (BBSs) such as CompuServe or GEnie.

Notes

Microsoft provides Windows NT support on
CompuServe, GEnie, BIX, WIX, and other networks.

If your SCSI adapter is not supported, and you need to
install Windows NT, check the documentation for
instructions on how to install Windows NT from a
network. This installation technique often enables you
to circumvent this problem, and it usually can be
performed on a single machine by treating a directory
on your drive as a network directory. You need lots of
free space on your drive, however, to use this technique.

Problem: *Windows NT starts, but then the system locks up.*

Steps To Follow

1.   Check for base memory address or interrupt
     request line conflicts in your hardware setup. Make
     sure that no two devices share an address or
     interrupt request.

2.   Run Setup again, and check that you have the
     correct video device driver installed.

3.   Turn on your printer. Some multiple I/O cards
     create a conflict with other devices—this action
     usually resolves the problem.

Program-Performance Problems

Problem: *The mouse pointer and open windows jerk, rather than move smoothly across the screen.*

Steps To Follow

Use the Desktop icon in the Control Panel to check the **G**ranularity setting. Jerky mouse and window movements indicate that the setting is too high.

Problem: *The Windows NT display is at a lower resolution than the monitor is capable of displaying.*

Steps To Follow

You usually need a different display driver, which typically has a DRV extension. Check with the video adapter's manufacturer to see if a higher-resolution driver is available for Windows NT. You can install new drivers by using the Windows NT Setup application.

Problem: *Only some of the Windows NT applications use the full 256-color palette.*

Steps To Follow

Some aspects of Windows NT itself, such as the Clipboard, support 256 colors—if you have a display

adapter that is capable of displaying 256 colors and a
Windows NT display driver that supports the adapter
in 256-color mode. Windows NT applications may or
may not support 256 colors, depending on the application. In any case, you must still have a 256-color
adapter and driver to make use of this capability.

Problem: *Graphics saved to the Clipboard as a 256-color image appear in black-and-white the next time the file is opened.*

Steps To Follow

1. Clipboard and Paintbrush can cause palette prob-
    lems with certain display/driver combinations.
    Avoid the use of the Clipboard altogether, or do
    not use the **N**ew command to clear the display
    before you paste the 256-color image into Paint-
    brush. (The **N**ew command clears Paintbrush's
    palette, which contributes to the problem.)

2. Use the eraser tool instead of the **N**ew command
    to erase the image, then paste in the other image.
    If the image's colors change, open the source
    image in Paintbrush, erase everything with the
    eraser tool, then save it as a template image with a
    new name. Use the **P**aste command to insert the
    new image into the template image.

Program Manager Problems

Problem: *Double-clicking on a document item does not launch the parent application, even though an association exists.*

Steps To Follow

Add the application's directory to your personal PATH variable by using the System icon in the Control Panel. You can also specify the full path to the application in the Command Line text box in the Program Manager's Program Item Properties dialog box (use the File, Properties command). Windows NT probably cannot locate the executable file.

Problem: *The changes made within Program Manager are not saved from session to session.*

Steps To Follow

Use the Save Settings on Exit command in Program Manager's Options menu to save the settings.

Problem: *Program Manager starts as an icon instead of as a window.*

Steps To Follow

1. Make sure that Program Manager is running as a window when you exit.

2. If the **M**inimize on Use option on the Program Manager **O**ptions menu is checked, launching an application automatically on startup can force the Program Manager to an icon. If you have anything in the Startup group, for example, Program Manager is minimized.

Problem: *The icons displayed in Program Manager are too crowded.*

Steps To Follow

Select the Desktop icon in the Control Panel, and increase the **I**con Spacing value.

Problem: *I want to save the Program Manager configuration without exiting Windows NT.*

Steps To Follow

Use the Save Settings **N**ow option on the Program Manager's Options menu.

Problem: *I want to use different spacings for icons within different group document windows.*

Steps To Follow

1. Set the **I**con Spacing from the Desktop icon in the Control Panel.

2. Select the group you want to space in the Program Manager.

3. Use the **A**rrange Icons option of the **W**indow
    menu to respace the icons.

4. Repeat the procedure for other groups, and save
    the Program Manager's settings.

Printing Problems

Problem: *The Print command is dimmed.*

Steps To Follow

You may not have installed a printer when you installed Windows NT. Start the Control Panel, and
double-click on the Printers icon. (Follow the procedure for adding a printer in Chapter 11). Make sure
that a printer appears in the default printer text box
when you are done.

Problem: *Windows NT does not include a printer driver for my printer.*

Steps To Follow

1. Check your printer manual to see whether it is
    compatible with one of Windows NT's existing
    printer drivers. Many dot-matrix printers are
    compatible with the IBM Graphics driver or the
    Epson driver. Laser printers are sometimes compat-
    ible with the HP LaserJet driver. Install the driver
    that the manual indicates is compatible.

2. If your manual does not indicate that the printer is
    compatible with one of the drivers available in
    Windows NT, call the manufacturer or supplier to
    see if a Windows NT driver is available for your
    printer.

Problem: *Printer documents are garbled or do not look right.*

Steps To Follow

1. You may have several printers installed, and have selected the wrong one as the active printer. Use the Printers icon in the Control Panel or the Print Manager to select the correct printer.

2. Some settings in your printer driver may be set inappropriately. Use the P**r**int Setup option from an application's **F**ile menu to verify that your driver's settings are set to the values you need.

Problem: *The correct printer driver is installed, the driver is active, and the printer is configured correctly, but the printer is still not working.*

Steps To Follow

1. Check for hardware problems: the power is on, paper is present, and a ribbon is installed.

2. Power down your computer. Ensure that the printer cable is properly connected to both the printer and the computer.

DOS, OS/2, and POSIX Applications Problems

Problem: *My application does not run properly.*

Steps To Follow

Some DOS, OS/2, and POSIX applications may not run properly because of Windows NT security. For security reasons, Windows NT does not give an application direct access to hardware devices. In other operating systems, there are often techniques by which programmers can speed up applications by bypassing the operating system and writing directly to the hardware.

Although the Windows NT design team tried to accommodate all of these programming techniques, they valued security over 100%-compatibility. Applications that do not run properly under the DOS, OS/2, and POSIX subsystems that are part of Windows NT probably use unsupported programming techniques.

Under these circumstances, keep both operating systems on your computer so that you can run your applications until the manufacturers provide Windows NT-compatible versions.

Index

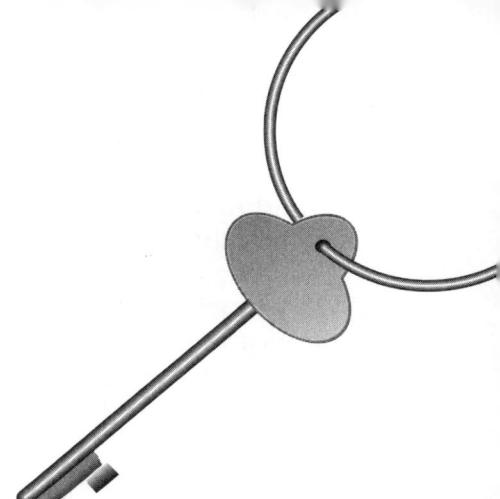

WANT MORE INFORMATION?

CHECK OUT THESE RELATED TITLES:

7 Keys To
Learning Windows NT
REGISTRATION CARD

Fill out this card to receive information about future 7 Keys books and other New Riders titles!

Name _____ **Title** _____

Company _____

Address _____

City/State/ZIP _____

I bought this book because _____
_____

I purchased this book from:
☐ A bookstore (Name _____)
☐ A software or electronics store (Name _____)
☐ A mail order (Name of Catalog _____)

I purchase this many computer books each year:
☐ 1–5   ☐ 5 or more

I currently use these applications: _____
_____
_____
_____

I found these chapters to be the most informative: _____
_____

I found these chapters to be the least informative: _____
_____

Additional comments: _____
_____

☐ I would like to see my name in print! You may use my name and quote me in future New Riders products and promotions. My daytime phone number is:_____

New Riders Publishing 11711 North College Avenue • P.O. Box 90 • Carmel, Indiana 46032 USA

------------------------------ Fold Here ------------------------------

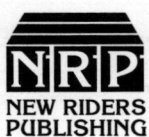

New Riders Publishing
11711 North College Avenue
P.O. Box 90
Carmel, Indiana 46032
USA